MAGNIFY THE LORD

MAGNIFY
THE LORD

Elaine Storkey

with a Foreword by the
Archbishop of Canterbury

Fount
An Imprint of HarperCollins*Publishers*

Fount is an Imprint of
HarperCollins*Religious*
Part of HarperCollins*Publishers*
77–85 Fulham Palace Road, London W6 8JB

First published in Great Britain
in 1993 by Fount Paperbacks under
the title *Mary's Story, Mary's Song*

Quotations from Scripture marked (NRSV) are taken from the
New Revised Standard Version Bible, Copyright © 1989,
Division of Christian Education of the
National Council of the Churches of Christ in the
United States of America

A catalogue record for this book is
available from the British Library

ISBN 0 00 628081 1

Printed and bound in Great Britain by
Caledonian International Book Manufacturing, Glasgow

To my own kinswomen,
Anne, my mother, Elizabeth my sister,
    and my cousins
Pat, June, Gillian, Susan and Yvonne

and my kinswomen through marriage
especially Helen, my daughter-in-law,
    Doris, my mother-in-law,
sisters-in-law Pat and Maxine

CONTENTS

FOREWORD

It is a privilege to be able to recommend *Magnify the Lord*. In it Elaine Storkey has brought much of her own experience and expertise to bear on a subject which is obviously close to her heart. Her gifts as counsellor, academic, debater, mother and believer combine together in a most exciting way. Her concern is to make Mary's story come alive to each one of us and to go on from there to ask how we can use it to serve as an example for our lives today.

Views about Mary have very sadly often been a cause of division amongst Christians. A biblical perspective asks that Mary's example should be an encouragement and a challenge to us all. From that moment when she responded to an angel to the great cadences of the Magnificat, this book opens up fresh insights into her life. The chapters need to be read slowly and their implications carefully weighed. Whether individually or as a member of a study group may I commend this book to you, and in Mary's own words, through it may you discover more about the 'God who fills the hungry with good things'.

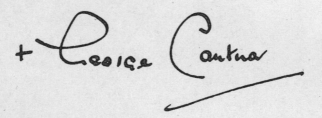

+ George Cantuar

INTRODUCTION

Contrary to popular wisdom, familiarity can breed delight. I found this when I focused once again on the first chapter of the Luke's Gospel to write this short book. It has been an exciting task to get inside the events which Luke records in a much more involved way. The richness of his account, in both style and detail, has always gripped me, but this time the depth and speed of the narrative had me particularly enthralled. The visit of the angel, the reunion of two cousins, the sharing of pregnancy, and the magnificent cadences of the Magnificat all come together as a satisfying whole in the story leading up to the birth of Christ. The fact that the chapter focuses largely on two women has become of special significance as I have grown in my own spiritual life. It is consciously as a woman that I have written this series of reflections and prayers upon the passage.

It is evident that in this chapter the Bible is speaking in many different ways. First, it speaks as *narrative*, for Luke is telling a story. I have tried to tell that story again, and look at its enormous relevance for our world today. Then, the Bible speaks here as *song*, for what Mary utters is indeed a wonderful song of praise, drawing together her own heritage and tradition in a new way. Then the Bible speaks as *history*, for the events described are not myth or fantasy, but provide the historical bedrock of our creeds and our faith. And the Bible also speaks as *prophecy*, for Mary both recalls the greatness of God throughout the ages, and also looks prophetically to what is yet to come. Finally the Bible speaks as *mystery,* for there are things

---

here too great for us ever to begin to comprehend without wisdom from the Holy Spirit. There is much in this short chapter which therefore draws us into the richness of the Bible as a whole. My ambition is to encourage you to read on, into the gospel of Luke and beyond, perhaps even recording your own meditations on what you find there.

The book falls into two natural halves. The first four chapters deal with events and observations before the Song begins; the other ten chapters each looks at an aspect of God as revealed in the Magnificat. Each individual chapter is short and bite-sized, so they can be read on brief journeys, during lunch breaks, or in any spare moments of a busy life. Or, for more sustained study three or more chapters can be taken together. The prayers which end each section are my own personal response to God. Where your experience is different you may sometimes want to write your own prayer, and clip it into the text.

Acknowledgements

I am grateful to many people for supporting this project. First to those people who have kindly allowed me to tell their stories in the pages of this book. In each case details have been changed to preserve confidentiality. The first edition came as a suggestion from the Archbishop of Canterbury and I remain in his debt for that. It benefited too from the kindness of the Dean of Carlisle who helpfully lent me material from his own library. My sons, Amos, Matthew and Caleb supported the project throughout and improved my computer literacy. My father, James Lively, kindly read the proofs. I am indebted to James Catford for his encouragement and suggestions for the revisions and commitment to seeing the book back in print. Susan Beresford, who runs my office at the Institute for Contemporary Christianity, has helped on this second edition, and for that and so much more I am grateful to her. My husband, Alan, has borne the biggest effects of the demands of writing. He, as always, has gone the extra mile, taking on a dozen things to make my life more manageable. To him and to everyone I say thank you.

In the sixth month the angel Gabriel was sent by God to a town in Galilee called Nazareth, to a virgin engaged to a man whose name was Joseph, of the house of David. The virgin's name was Mary. And he came to her and said, 'Greetings, favoured one! The Lord is with you.' But she was much perplexed by his words and pondered what sort of greeting this might be. The angel said to her, 'Do not be afraid, Mary, for you have found favour with God. And now, you will conceive in your womb and bear a son, and you will name him Jesus. He will be great, and will be called the Son of the Most High, and the Lord God will give him the throne of his ancestor David. He will reign over the house of Jacob forever, and of his kingdom there will be no end.' Mary said to the angel, 'How can this be, since I am a virgin?' The angel said to her, 'The Holy Spirit will come upon you, and the power of the Most High will overshadow you; therefore the child to be born will be holy; he will be called Son of God. And now, your relative Elizabeth in her old age has also conceived a son; and this is the sixth month for her who was said to be barren. For nothing will be impossible with God.' Then Mary said, 'Here am I, the servant of the Lord; let it be with me according to your word.' Then the angel departed from her.

In those days Mary set out and went with haste to a Judean town in the hill country, where she entered the house of Zechariah and greeted Elizabeth. When Elizabeth heard Mary's greeting, the child leaped in her womb. And Elizabeth was filled with the Holy Spirit and exclaimed with a loud cry, 'Blessed are you among women, and blessed is the fruit of your womb. And why has this happened to me, that the mother of my Lord comes to me? For as soon as I heard the sound of your greeting, the child in my womb leaped for joy. And blessed is she who believed that there would be a fulfillment of what was spoken to her by the Lord.'

And Mary said,

'My soul magnifies the Lord, and my spirit rejoices in God my Saviour, for he has looked with favour on the lowliness of his servant. Surely, from now on all generations will call me blessed; for the Mighty One has done great things for me, and holy is his name. His mercy is for those who fear him from generation to generation. He has shown strength with his arm; he has scattered the proud in the thoughts of their hearts. He has brought down the powerful from their thrones, and lifted up the lowly; he has filled the hungry with good things, and sent the rich away empty. He has helped his servant Israel, in remembrance of his mercy, according to the promise he made to our ancestors, to Abraham and to his descendants forever.'

And Mary remained with her about three months and then returned to her home.

(NRSV) Luke 1:26–55

ONE

GOD'S INITIATIVE

LUKE 1: 35–38

The angel said to her, 'The Holy Spirit will come upon you and the power of God will overshadow you: so that the baby born to you will be utterly holy – the Son of God. And your cousin Elizabeth, called the barren one, has also become pregnant in her old age. For with God nothing is impossible.' And Mary said, 'I am the servant of the Lord. May every thing happen to me just as you have said.'

A visit from an angel

However it is told the story of Mary is a remarkable one.

The modern tabloid newspapers could hardly dream up anything more sensational, more full of 'human interest', and more unlikely. An angel comes to a young woman and tells her she will become miraculously pregnant. The child which she is to bear will be the Son of God. In the short recorded encounter the woman has time to make only two responses. The first is: 'How is this likely?' – a predictable response indeed from someone who has never had sex with any man, and is not intending to until she is married. The second is far less predictable: 'Yes, I am willing for this to happen'.

The story is difficult for us today for many reasons. First, of course, we live in a world which would hardly know how to recognize an angel. Frankly, most of us do not believe in them. We can somehow believe in astrology, and take great interest in signs of the zodiac. We may believe in the demonic, or even dabble with witchcraft or the occult. Yet few of us expect visits from angels.

Perhaps it is that angels are too benign, too personal. They do not belong to a universe which accepts fatalism or chance. They do not remind us of evil and hatred. They are not part of the sinister, the pantheistic or the psychic. Compared with all of these, angels are fairly ordinary creatures who crop up unannounced in apparently everyday situations. They might be unlimited by the space-time boundaries which affect us mortals, but it would seem that they are otherwise quite average. In the Bible they busily flit between time and eternity as willing messengers sent from God. Today people find all of that hard to grasp hold of. For the modern mind is very perverse. Some people find it easier to believe that their next Tuesday morning will be affected by the relationship of Jupiter and Saturn on the day they were born, than to believe in a God who cares about us. So it seems doubly hard for some people to believe in angels. For if we accept that angels exist, we have to accept that there is a God who has been sending them to communicate with human beings for the last few thousand years. We might also have to accept the possibility that God could do that even today.

A second problem with the story is Mary's own reaction. From what we have to go on, it seems strange indeed to contemporary ears that she should change so rapidly from incredulous surprise to willing acquiescence. Why should she? Yet this is less surprising when we consider the understanding which Mary brings to her visit from the angel. For what lies between her two responses is a depth of belief, awareness and commitment which is almost absent from our modern mind-set. With Mary there is a fundamental acceptance that we live in a world which is not controlled by human design or human whim. At the very centre of the universe is a Creator God, who makes everything that is alive: the cells in our bodies, the ebbing and flowing tide, the sap rising in the tree. The whole of this reality is upheld by God's Word of power. And this

Creator is in close touch with the creation, for God is the author of everything in it. We ourselves are God's handiwork, moulded and created in God's image, and it is God who breathes in us the very breath of life. This is the belief context in which Mary hears the angel's message.

So unlike the way we might react, Mary does not question the angel either about his own existence or about the existence of God. For the reality of God's existence has been the lifelong context for her daily experiences. From her childhood she has heard the psalms, the law and the prophets. She has been taught that God is her Maker, the rock of her people, the protector, the strong tower. She has heard God likened to a mother eagle giving warmth and nurture to her chicks. She has known and believed that wisdom and truth come from God alone. She has seen and believed that the heavens tell out God's glory and that the earth shows God's handiwork. Having lived in a reality disclosed by the word of God, and refreshed by the presence of God, Mary does not need to be convinced on this score. This much she takes for granted in the angel's visit.

Nor does Mary question the angel about the news that Messiah will come. For as a young Jewish woman she stands in a long line of praying men and women who have longed for the redemption promised by God, Yahwe. She shares the yearning of all Israel, indeed of all humanity, for restoration: to know wholeness in the very depths of being, and to talk peacefully before the face of God. And she knows the promise of deliverance which has echoed down the centuries: that Yahwe will again visit his people to bring forgiveness and healing. There is so much in Mary's culture which tells her to watch and pray for the coming kingdom. Nothing the angel says about the coming of the Holy One produces any problem for belief.

Yet Mary does have a question for the angel. For not all she has heard seems right. What Mary finds difficult to grasp is her own part in this amazing event. She is taken completely off her guard by the very suggestion that she is herself somehow central to God's plans, that she has been chosen as the one through whom God will fulfil his promise. So her question comes not from doubt or uncertainty, but from the great wealth of trust she has in God. Why ever should she be entrusted with bringing into being the longed-for one of Israel? Can the angel be certain? The very possibility of any pregnancy seems unlikely, let alone a pregnancy which stands at the crossroads of God's covenantal history. For even if God were to choose such a very ordinary woman she herself would seem an unlikely candidate. For she is unmarried, completely untutored in sexuality, and has not yet given childbirth a moment's thought.

In this question Mary reflects the third difficulty we have today with the story. Contemporary people find it very hard to believe that a woman who never had sexual intercourse could ever have had a baby. And on this score the angel explains very little to his surprised listener. He says neither why nor how these events will take place; makes little attempt to analyse the extraordinary process about to happen. The answer is woefully brief. For his modern critics his account of conception is very unsatisfying. To the sceptical minds of our age it is inadequate in the extreme. There is no information about how God intends to implant male sperm to fertilize a female egg. There is no discussion of genes or chromosomes. It is extremely inconsiderate of the angel not to think of us at the end of the second millennium and to anticipate our need for detailed and accurate understanding. Luke, the recorder of the gospel, could at least have managed an aside or a footnote. Of course many people today become very patronizing towards the biblical writers for their lack of modern knowledge. And certainly obstetrics and gynaecology were in their infancy. But the good doctor Luke knew even then that women do not become mysteriously pregnant outside normal sex. Yet the faithful scribe records only the bare details of what the angel said: that the Holy Spirit of God was to come upon Mary and she would be overshadowed by the power of the Most High. How frustrating this is for many of his modern readers, who wish that he would have taken some time and effort to reassure us about the scientific possibility of the Virgin Birth!

And yet of course even if the angel had been able to explain the process in detail, neither Mary nor we would have been able to understand it. For what the angelic messenger was sent to communicate was far beyond the capacities of finite, human thought. Our most brilliant equations, calculations or formulae look like childish scribble on a nursery colouring book, alongside the divine thought which went into planning this unique pregnancy. For the same God who, in those poetic words to Job, showed the dawn its place, led the eagle to safety, and gave birth to the ice and frost, now conceives a Son to be born as human flesh in a human body. And we, with our puny intellect, feel affronted if God has not deigned to take us into the cosmic intricacies of the divine plan. If we do not understand it, we will not believe it. If we cannot master (or mistress) it by our intellect then we will deride it as ridiculous. But once we have abolished all mystery and fulfilled our own need for rationalistic certainty we will still live in a world which lacks explanation. For as the psalmist observed with characteristic humility: the fear of God is the beginning of wisdom.

So many of our contemporary difficulties with the story arise because we exalt our limited and mortal minds and do not realize how very little we know. And so those clever sceptics of today who would rather believe in their own limited understanding are less wise than this young Jewish woman of two thousand years before. Her readiness to listen, her depth of awareness of God and her responses of obedience conveyed something of the reality within which she lived. Her reply to the angelic messenger indicated that she knew the source of knowledge and truth, and that it did not lie with arrogant humans. 'I am the Lord's servant', she replied. 'May it be to me as you have said.'

The servant of the Lord

Mary could not have accepted the role of servant if she had not first abandoned her own autonomy: the 'right' to live her life independently of the call of God or the needs of others. And it is the demands of human independence which lie behind so many of our problems of unbelief today. Not only do we reserve the right to have everything brought within our intellectual autonomy, we also insist on the right to our own moral and personal autonomy. We draw up our own agendas. We live with our own decisions. We write our own scripts. If a given morality does not suit us, we change it. If our friends are too demanding, we drop them. We try our hardest to construct a world which assures us that we can live the way we want, that we are what we have, and that truth is what we say it is. And then we wonder why we cannot believe in God.

Mary shared none of these assumptions. Although she could presumably have rejected the angel's story and refused her assent to the proposal, she did not. With this young, believing Jewish woman there was no question of living life according to her own rules or requirements. For even if this were possible (and few even today are any longer convinced by this myth) her life would be the poorer, not the richer as a result.

To be the 'servant of the Lord' has enormous implications for anyone. It means nothing less than death to self; giving up our own small ambitions, putting ourselves at God's disposal. It requires an abandonment of pride and the acceptance of a more humble assessment of ourselves. It means also embracing others as our equals. For the implications of servanthood are mutuality and acceptance. The joy is that when servanthood is welcomed eagerly, excitedly, then the death we must die to all more superficial ways of existing and relating becomes easier. For servanthood is not something we choose in opposition to rich independence. It is something we choose in opposition to self-centred arrogance and toil.

As for the young pregnant virgin who was already of low worldly status, becoming the Lord's servant was to take away even that respect that she had in the eyes of her society. It was to involve misunderstanding and possible ostracism. It was to strain relations with her fiancé, who would need his own visit from the angel to assure him that there had been no infidelity. Now there would be a need to take fast action, a quick marriage, some legal protection. Unless Joseph were to accept her as his wife, there would be wagging tongues indeed when Mary returned from her three-month visit to cousin Elizabeth. For even under the loose robes of the Middle East there is a limit to what can be passed off as an increase in weight.

Being the Lord's servant was to change the course of Mary's whole life. She was to know the unease of being an unmarried pregnant mother, the discomfort of hard travelling close to childbirth and the difficulties of labour under extreme conditions. She was to experience anxiety when, at the age of twelve, her much-loved son disappears from the travelling party. She was to know the contentment of seeing him come into manhood, and maternal pride and satisfaction as he brings joy and healing to others. She was to suffer bewilderment as he spurns the requests of the family and allows the needs of others to come first. She was to endure fear and terror as he is indicted on a trumped-up charge, and dragged from courtroom to courtroom. And there can be little to match her experience of utter devastation, grief and loneliness as she watches his agonizing death. When she gives her answer to the angel Mary can be only dimly aware of all that it will draw her into, and of the emotional pain such a response will bring. As the servant-mother of the Lord she will have her own cross to bear, her own deep thoughts to keep and ponder in her heart.

God's call is never tidy or predictable. This young Jewish woman could have expected an uncomplicated life as the eventual wife of a respected local carpenter, but instead she takes on dimensions of responsibility, apprehension, fear and grief which she and Joseph had probably never thought possible in their early days of betrothal. Yet the initiating God called Mary into servanthood and Mary responded. What was to follow was not hers to control, but was in the hands of God. What was within her control was just the willingness to accept the task she was being called to do.

The underlying pattern of the call to servanthood is a simple one and has been repeated over and over again. The process of God's calling and our responding has echoed down the centuries. Many have found that this call has seized hold of their own well-planned lives, and taken them to places they never dreamed of, or into experiences and excitement which was unimaginable. Others have found that the call has entailed separation and loss and suffering they never thought endurable. Today God still initiates a movement of the Holy Spirit in individual people's lives, and asks them to become servants of the Most High.

Yet, although she was not alone in being called of God, the weight which lay on Mary's response is in one sense unparalleled, for so much depended on it. A young and very ordinary Jewish woman was asked to be involved in something which was to change the future of the world. This is one of the mysteries of our faith, that the God who is Almighty and Sovereign over the whole of creation has yet given to human beings the power to accept or reject his invitation to us. God does not batter us into submission, but just asks us to choose this day whom we will serve. The Holy Spirit is there to help us, yet God leaves to us the choice we will make. The very process feels risky. And in this case the risk seems enormous. Resting on Mary's reply was the weight of history, the weight of eternity, the weight of God's planned redemption for the whole creation groaning in its lostness. Her simple response: 'May it be to me as you have said' was truly a response uttered through the power of the Spirit. It was all that God required to set into action the most cosmic event since the creation of the universe itself. And the world would receive its Messiah.

Prayer

God of all wisdom and knowledge.

Help us to realize that, although your ways are not our ways
And your thoughts are not your thoughts,
And there stretches between us the great gulf of our mortality,
You have plans for us.
And our little knowledge will be no hindrance to our progress,
Our limited intellect will not cause us to stumble,
When we walk in faith and obedience
With you. Amen.

Questions

1 When there are so many references to angels in both the Old and the
 New Testaments, why do you think we pay so little attention to
 them in the Church today?
2 Why is servanthood a difficult thing to accept in our modern world,
 even when it is with regard to God?

TWO

GOD'S LEADING

LUKE 1:39–40

At that time Mary got ready and hurried to a town in the hill country of Judea, where she entered Zechariah's home and greeted Elizabeth. Now as soon as Elizabeth heard Mary's greeting the child leapt in her womb and Elizabeth was filled with the Holy Spirit. In a loud voice she exclaimed: 'Blessed are you among women and blessed is the child you will bear! But why am I so favoured that the mother of my Lord should come to me?'

There is nothing new about pregnant women getting together to share the anticipation of motherhood, especially when they are both carrying their first children. Cousins especially have a strong link. For they are family together, not sisters but have that one-remove which brings a comfortable, relaxed relationship born out of many years of bonding. These cousins had something very special to share. Not only were their pregnancies both unexpected, they each had the knowledge that God's own miraculous power had been involved. Elizabeth was well known as past childbearing age. For years she had felt diminished as a woman when the hallmark of womanly success had been to produce a quiver full of children for a proud husband. So not only her own status but that of Zechariah had suffered in their childlessness. The stigma of infertility is not of course limited to those times. Our contemporary society offers pity and medical aids, but those who cannot bear children still often feel on the outside of a successful breeding population. In her day Elizabeth experienced overt reproach and scorn from other women. She was referred to as the 'barren woman', a cruel reminder from others of her ineffectualness and inadequacy. There must

15

have been times when she felt very close to Hannah in the Hebrew scriptures: that other childless woman of long before who had prayed fervently in the Temple and pleaded with God for a child. And now, as it did with Hannah, everything had changed. The past few months had taught her that what God had promised was really going to happen. The child inside her was growing strong and lively and making his presence felt. Even her cynical husband had been silenced, and the next words he uttered would be of praise, joy, prophecy and blessing. And so now Elizabeth cannot wait to see her cousin. Soon she will confirm with her own eyes what she knows already by faith, and Mary will have her own story affirmed in Elizabeth's blessing. There is indeed so much for the two women to share. As one author comments, with gentle insight: 'One is old and has no children; the other is young and has no husband. But both are pregnant. God, Hannah's God, has been at work.'[1] The women embrace each other in growing realization of the miraculous power of this God, full of awe and amazement that two ordinary cousins should have been given such an extraordinary blessing.

Mary and Elizabeth are linked in a long line of women who share together and bless each other.

The old teaches and nurtures the young, and receives from her in return the joy of newness and insights full of fresh vision. The young follows and reveres the old, and sustains her with youthful protection and energy for the next part of the journey. Mother-daughter, grandmother-granddaughter all share the strengths and vulnerabilities of being women, knowing often without words the lives and emotions of the other. Even in our individualized societies today women can break free from the prevailing self-sufficiency and acknowledge an enriching interdependence. Sisters and cousins can show deep care for each other and others within the family. Neighbours and friends can share mutual needs and receive openly from each other. Nurses and teachers, businesswomen and students can live their lives co-operatively as women, releasing and energizing those they serve. Labourers and workers, whether in American offices, African fields or Asian factories all have within their power the ability to encourage and enhance the lives of others who work with them. Womanpower is not a secularized force discovered in the heady days of the 1970s. It is what God has breathed into the creation, and it is there for sustenance, enrichment and care.

We can see this echoed so often in the pages of Scripture, for Mary and Elizabeth stand also in a line of many biblical women who reach out to each other in faithfulness and blessing. Once we have eyes to see them they tumble out of history and live again in the ever-freshness of God's Word. We can read their fascinating stories: of the midwives in Exodus who refused the orders of Pharaoh to abort the Israelite babies, because they knew what childbirth meant for those in labour pangs; of Miriam and her mother, together protecting the child in the first Moses basket in the bullrushes, listening to each other's fears and learning wisdom and quick thinking from the other; of Ruth and Naomi, committed passionately to each other, staying firm in their love and allegiance, and bringing blessings to the whole of Israel. Or we can turn to those women in the New Testament who follow the same tradition. We can listen to the lives of Mary and Martha, those sisters who loved each other and the Christ who raised their brother from the dead. We can learn of Susanna and Joanna who supported Jesus financially, travelling with him on that final journey, and making a gloriously abortive trip to anoint his body on the resurrection day. We can ponder over Euodia and Syntyche, those committed women leaders in the early Church who in spite of all their loyalty and hard work for the Gospel still struggled to be reconciled after a difficult dispute. God has populated the Scriptures with faithful, loving women who are committed to be servants of each other and of God. The encounter between Mary and Elizabeth recalls them all and touches into the depths of women's experiences throughout the ages.

Leaving home for a journey

Before the encounter can take place Mary has to leave home and make a journey. And this raises an interesting point: who told Mary to make such a journey? The gospel writer does not let us know why Mary visited Elizabeth or why she should undertake this difficult piece of travel at a vulnerable time during early pregnancy. There is certainly no indication that she was instructed to do so by the angel. It would seem that she was left to make her own decisions, to live as seemed best to her before God. And in that she shares the experiences of the majority of us. Most of us are not regularly instructed by angels. More normally God leaves us to discern the leading of the Holy Spirit ourselves, through prayer, through listening, through compassion or through plain commonsense. It is the prompting of these that sets Mary off on her journey. As a young woman pregnant out of wedlock, she is not running away from her family in shame. She knows that what is happening to her is miraculous, and she turns to the person in her family who can give her spiritual help and advice. She goes to her older cousin for wisdom and understanding. But she goes too to bring physical help with her. Elizabeth is much older. Her needs are different from Mary's, and she can use the support and help of the younger woman. So Mary does not spend time agonising about where she might find advice, or how she might best help her cousin. She hears Elizabeth's news and packs her bags. As one commentator observes: 'Mary goes, not consciously to bring Christ to another. She merely reaches out to another in need.'[2] Very often God does not expect us to wait until we have absolute certainty that a particular way forward is God's will for our lives. Instead we are expected to take risks, to reach out in faith and trust that God will make our path increasingly plain as we walk along it.

Like Ruth with Naomi then, Mary has to leave home. She must go from her familiar and much-loved surroundings and travel for the sake of the older woman. And this is no doubt costly. There is the arduous demand of the journey itself before facing the requirement to adjust to the rhythm of life in a new area. There is the absence of familiar faces, the loss of comforting landmarks. Leaving home, if only for three months, can be a difficult experience.

Emotionally, this is no easier today, when jet planes shrink the globe and enable us to cross continents in less time than Mary took to go from Galilee to the hill country of Judea. There is always that sense of going away, even temporarily, from roots which go long and deep. My own early days of leaving home were inevitably mixed with both excitement and sorrow, whether it was to my first school holiday, to university in Wales, or to a year of research in Canada. There was the fascination of doing new things, seeing new faces, visiting new locations. Yet I would be leaving behind precious people with whom I would have so liked to share these experiences. For their lives had surrounded mine from my earliest years, filling it with warmth and security; they loved me dearly and wished me well. By the time I left home to marry Alan and create a new home, I had become practised in the art of separation, though it was still not without pain. Yet it was only when I too became a mother and watched my eldest son leave home for university that I understood the cost to my own mother each time, in generously letting me go.

Travelling away is even more difficult, however, if we have never had a home to go from. As one writer has observed: 'We cannot set out on a journey unless we first have a place to leave.' Mary had the security of her rootedness in Nazareth, and people to leave behind. The importance of a home base was very much a feature of the Jewish culture. The allocation of land, the requirements of hospitality, the provisions for the alien or the stranger were all woven into the way God asked the Israelites to live; the relationship with home echoes throughout the Hebrew Scriptures. Sometimes in the biblical narrative God did of course call people to a nomadic existence, yet this was almost always a communal calling, or a temporary one. It was often so that those called might be more reliant on God. Sometimes it required a time of preparation; frequently it involved a sense of loss. When the Israelites were sent wandering in the wilderness there was great impatience and heartache when the promised land did not yet materialize. God's call to be homeless was never to be rootless. It still required the leaving of somewhere which had been home. The sense of place was now replaced by the sense of community, and the people were asked to be a place to each other. They were also asked to put down deeper roots in God.

Our present culture offers confused images of home. Too many people grow up knowing no true home, or one which does not ground them in love. A childhood spent with no real sense of location is a poor preparation for a secure adulthood. For much of our personal identity and our secure sense of self comes from our childhood context, and from those who made it our own special place. Low self-esteem, self-hatred, inability to accept the love of others also have their roots so often in early childhood influences. For some of us grew up among those who were not able to show us our true value and worth.

Our present culture also does much damage to people through its rootlessness. Three groups of people particularly suffer in our stranded societies today. The first are the homeless themselves. Increasingly the only home many people know is a cardboard box on a street pavement, or in a subway tunnel. In Britain in 1993 it was estimated that 9,000 would be sleeping rough on any one night. Some of these have been without a place not for months but for years. Many have run away from 'care' when they were children; others split from partners, drop out and end up on the streets. In some countries outside Europe the problem is yet greater, and the homeless figures would include many more children. A year ago I visited Salvador in Brazil and, like many before me, found it hard to come to terms with the large number of children abandoned to the streets of the city. If they were asked where their 'casa' (the Portuguese for home) was, most of them would not know what was meant. They got their food by begging or stealing, and spent much time avoiding the roughness and recriminations of the police. No nurturing, no education, no care about standards of health or morality left many of these children defenceless against malnutrition, disease and exploitation. By the time they had grown into puberty the street children themselves would be having their own children, who in turn would be brought up on the streets or abandoned at birth. For me it was a great relief to meet a Belgian priest who had gone to minister in one of the poorest parts of the city. I spent a day in his children's shelter and school, where hundreds of children, from infancy to adolescence, found a daily home. The detailed care, medical help, teaching, and daily nurture which the Brazilian Sisters gave in the name of Christ supported whatever family these children already had, and meant that they were not among the abandoned ones. In other cities the missionaries from the South American Missionary Society worked with the children out on the streets, bringing both food, help and care along with the hope of the Gospel. Creating the reality of home for the homeless is one of the most urgent tasks facing the Church today.

It is not only the technically homeless, however, who have no home. Many others have grown up knowing no stable surroundings. For some people 'home' is where they were abused, or constantly criticized, or used as movable pieces in tragic adult games. Children who have spent all their years of childhood being moved from one foster home to another, or from one care order to another, find it difficult to make their own journeys through life. This came home to me again recently when I counselled the wife of a man who was incapable of giving anything of himself, either to her or to their child. His infancy and childhood had been spent in fifteen different local authority homes, punctuated with periods in hospitals then followed by the uncertainty of which foster home might take him next. From the age of sixteen he had lived on his own in several bedsits. He met his wife in his twenties, when the woman and her mother had been trying to coax their bewildered and frightened puppy off the ice in the local park. With characteristic concern for a creature in trouble he came to the rescue, earning the long-term friendship of the dog. The couple fell in love and married quite quickly. Marriage had become a struggle from the time their son was born, but she was prepared to be patient, knowing his 'good side' and believing that ultimately this would flourish. Yet as the years passed, whilst he was moderately successful in business, his deep-rooted insecurity turned sour and into great bitterness. He criticized his wife and son incessantly, especially when they generously gave time or money to others. If anything came his way he would grab at it, clutch it to himself as though someone might just be waiting to wrench it out of his grasp. He could never let go of anything, and tried to fill his life with things, because he had earned them and they were his. Yet he was unable to put down any emotional roots, either in his marriage or in their home. He never found any sense of place. They moved constantly from one house to another, looking for somewhere better to settle. He could not settle anywhere new, because he had never had anywhere to leave behind. Instead, his loneliness and rootlessness went with him on every journey, and eventually wrecked his marriage.

This sad story and so many others illustrate how much those early experiences in our personal context affect us throughout our lives. Sister Elizabeth Ruth Obbard puts it strongly: 'A person who is "at home" in the place of his childhood is "at home" anywhere.'³ Yet the Christian message is not a fatalist one. Our thinking need never fall into a deterministic spiral. For even if our homes have not given us any of that constant, unconditional love which helps us to understand better the love of God, there is no need for despair. Although a good experience of home is of immeasurable benefit, God's love can break through the worst childhood history. The message of Christian hope is available also for the rootless. In the power of Christ people can cut away the bondage of a destructive past and tap down into yet deeper roots of love and care. For our real home is with God, and that home travels with us. It is always more abiding and permanent than our home with anyone else. And the journey which begins when we become disciples of Christ continues whatever our place and background. And whether or not it involves us in a physical move from any place, it will require us to be constantly leaving things behind and reach out to what is yet to come. St Paul sums this up so well in his letter to the Philippian church when he talks of his own journey: 'This one thing I do, forgetting what lies behind, and straining towards what is ahead, I press on towards the goal to win the prize for which God has called me heavenwards in Christ Jesus.'

In making her own journey, then, Mary also left what lay behind and pressed on to the goal given her by God. She went out in security and peace, both physically taking leave of the place she loved, and also taking leave of her plans of the past. In a very clear and powerful way the journey was to symbolize a new beginning.

Hospitality

Hospitality is at the centre of the story of the cousins' visit. Elizabeth's home becomes Mary's home, and the two share their lives together at a deep point in their walk with God. They eat together and rest together, they rejoice with each other and recall God's goodness to them. For hospitality means more than making someone welcome. It is that state of heart, that willingness to enter into the presence of another and be made at home. With great insight and perception Henri Nouwen talks about the intrinsic link between hospitality and poverty: when we have nothing we are the best hosts:

It is the paradox of hospitality that poverty makes a good host. Poverty is the inner disposition that allows us to take away our defences and convert our enemies into friends. We can only perceive the stranger as an enemy as long as we have something to defend. But when we say, 'Please enter – my house is your house, my joy is your joy, my sadness is your sadness and my life is your life' we have nothing to defend, since we have nothing to lose but all to give.[4]

There is therefore no automatic guarantee that when people get together there will be real hospitality. All too often, even though we long for human encounter, something of our own insecurity or reservation, or fear of becoming vulnerable prevents us from showing or receiving the openheartedness without which hospitality is impossible. How many times do people get together with others, and come away disappointed? There has been plenty to eat or drink, there has been music and talk. But there has not been encounter. There has been too much to prove, too much to defend, too much to control. Hospitality was not with the host, and was not invited as a guest.

The visit recorded in this passage by Luke has an altogether different dimension. Mary goes to Elizabeth at Judea both to receive hospitality, and also to take it with her. Elizabeth, elderly and excited, has nothing to hide from her cousin. Her vulnerability and poverty are obvious. For years she has been made to feel inadequate. Now she could be thought of as ridiculous. No doubt her neighbours have questioned whether she really is going to have a baby, or is under some pathetic delusion. But the arrival of her younger cousin means she can share fully and hospitably all that God has given to her. And as Mary receives she also gives. Hospitality comes with her in her own

disclosure of herself. She is willing to have her story fully
exposed to Elizabeth's scrutiny, knowing that she will find
reciprocation and understanding. But Mary also brings
hospitality because she brings the Host himself. Though
only as an embryo, the very Word of God is already with
the cousins; hospitality comes with Mary in the new
Person who has taken up residence within her.

Pregnancy itself is a symbol of deep hospitality. It is the
giving of one's body to the life of another. It is a sharing of all
that we have, our cell structure, our blood stream, our food,
our oxygen. It is saying 'welcome' with every breath, and
every heartbeat. And for many mothers that welcome is giv-
en irrespective of the demands made on one's comfort,
health or ease of life. For the demands of this hospitality are
greater than almost any of our own. And the growing foetus
is made to know that here is love, here are warm lodgings,
here is a place of safety. In hiding and in quiet the miraculous
growth can take place. 'In secret you knitted my parts
together in my mother's womb', whispered the psalmist. 'I
am fearfully and wonderfully made.' (Psalm 39:13–14)

This is one of the reasons why the decision for abortion
is such a painful and heavy one. Of course there are those
who have been taught by our culture to present themselves
to the clinic with barely a second thought, accepting the
sterile terminology of the hospital for what they are about
to do: 'a termination of pregnancy'. Yet for very many
other women who have had an abortion there has been
anxiety and grief and a sense of loss. In spite of all the reasons which directed them to take this step some feel guilty
of a deep betrayal of trust. They could not find within themselves the hospitality that was needed to sustain this life.

*

The two cousins had no such agonizing decisions to make.
They knew themselves to be utterly called by God to the

hospitality they were offering. They gave their bodies willingly to be inhabited by these new tiny persons, and were committed to nurturing and sustaining the children growing within them. Yet they knew also that the situations of their pregnancies were not the same. They were unalike, not only in the obvious way that Elizabeth was older and beyond normal childbearing years, and Mary was younger and unmarried when she conceived. They were different also in that the son Elizabeth was to bear would become the herald and prophet of the Son who was already forming in Mary's womb. So Elizabeth saw her own hospitality of receiving a guest as utterly overshadowed by the hospitality of Mary's coming to be with her. Her cry, 'Why should I be honoured with a visit from the mother of my Lord?' was an utterance given to her with all the clarity of the Holy Spirit. In that fraction of time that it took for Mary's greeting to reach her at the house, Elizabeth had become transformed. The reason for her own late conception was suddenly dawning upon her, along with the awesome realization that the two women stood together in the very presence of the Most High God. And Elizabeth's spirit rose within her to a powerful vision of happiness and truth.

The three months of hospitality which Mary and Elizabeth enjoyed together must have been times of great refreshment and peace. We get a powerful glimpse of their relationship, and their joy in each other's company when their mutual blessing and outpouring of praise to God is recorded for us by Luke. Yet what happens day by day as they go about the normal routines of life we do not know. No one has written down for us their many conversations, or the details of their relationships with other people. We are left only to imagine how they might have communicated with Zechariah, who had been deprived of his power of speech. We do not even know whether Mary stayed for Elizabeth's confinement, or whether she helped with the birth. What we do know is that here were two women, presented for us as a snapshot in a small flash of history, who loved, served and encouraged each other. In this tiny segment of recorded Christian memory we are able to see, as they never could, what effects their obedience and love would have on the history of the world. And in this fragment of living truth we can look back and also know, as they could not yet, what their obedience and hospitality would cost them as mothers.

Prayer

On our journey, Lord, we meet many travellers
Some are lonely, broken and depressed,
Unable to see the distant horizon because the past clouds their
    vision.
Others are complacent, self-satisfied,
Finding in their affluence and ease the resting place they want.
And yet your call continues,
Disturbing, persistent,
This is not our destination
Nor even where we stop awhile and stare with voyeuristic glee
At things which stimulate our sensations.
We are to be pilgrims, not tourists,
Reaching out, not giving in
Pressing onward, moving forward,
Journeying with measured step
Into your hospitality.

Questions

1 Many people think of one particular place as home even when they no longer live there. What is home for you and why?

2 What do you think are the most important things about home life from a Christian point of view? How could the Church do more to help the different kinds of 'homeless' people?

3 What was the last big journey you made? Try to compare it with Mary's journey from Galilee to Judea.

THREE

GOD'S WITNESS

LUKE 1:41

As soon as the sound of your greeting reached my ears, the baby in my womb leaped for joy.

The reaction of the baby in the womb to the newcomer in Judea is a very significant one. Luke, the doctor, is interested enough in the detail to record it, not once but twice. He mentions it in the narrative itself, and then in the inspired words which Elizabeth utters. And of course, foetuses of a reasonable size do move around in the womb. They kick, wriggle and take up the most awkward positions for the mother. Mothers in Elizabeth's day, no less than today, would know about the way changes in size affect both mother and baby. It is more than likely that they too would accommodate themselves to getting whatever comfort they could. Yet what we know today and what Elizabeth would not have known is that babies in the womb are affected also by many psychological conditions. Detailed studies to which Luke would never have had access, tell us of the effects of fear and trauma, or the prolonged anxiety of the mother. They indicate the positive influence of maternal stability and tranquillity, and even identify external situations to which babies have shown sensitivity. The debate continues as to how far the terrifying wail of air-raid sirens or the heavy blast of bombs produces long-lasting effects for someone who experienced it all before birth.

So for a child to leap in the womb when something dramatic is happening is by no means unusual. Yet what Elizabeth describes is more than a natural reaction of a human foetus to some external stimulus. Her baby relates to the sound of Mary's greeting, and to the presence of Mary's own infant. The movement of this baby is a leap of joy. It is the recognition that although his eyes cannot yet see nor his lungs yet breathe this baby knows he is in the very presence of God. The Holy Spirit discloses to this unborn child that what is developing in the womb of Mary is none other than the coming Messiah. And the foetus inside Elizabeth gives his own gesture of praise and exhortation.

This should not really surprise us. So often the Bible reminds us that the truth of who God is can be grasped by tiny human beings. And small children can be fulsome indeed in their acknowledgement of God's glory. In Psalm 8 the writer notes in wonder: 'From the lips of babes and infants you have ordained praise', and Jesus refers to this psalm when he welcomes children to himself. The hearts of the very young can often grasp the reality and majesty of God in a clearer way than those of their elders. A childlike trust and simplicity of faith is often more apparent among those who have not yet learnt to be clever in their doubts and build a theology out of their scepticism.

There are examples of this in the Bible as well as in our own experience. Which of us has not been stirred by the story of Samuel, the lad born to Hannah, that other barren woman? For centuries adults and children have admired Hannah's faithfulness in letting Samuel go, still a child, to live and work in the Temple. Who knows what it cost her emotionally to fulfil her promise to give this wonderful answer to prayer back into the service of God? And who can guess how much her own childlike commitment influenced her young son, and made him completely open to God? Wherever it has been told, the account of Samuel in the Temple has gripped the imagination of millions. Children and adults have felt the tingle of excitement as Samuel runs backwards and forwards to old Eli the priest to find why he is being called during his time of sleep. And when Eli grasps what we already know, that it is the voice of God prompting the young lad, we wait with anticipation for the outcome. Samuel's obedient and reverent response, 'Speak, Lord, for your servant is listening', brings from God a sharing of the wisdom and truths which were hidden from the mature and worldly-wise. There is so much in the story that anticipates Christ's own observations about young human beings; so much that alerts us to his respect for their directness and trust. We would do well to ponder what Jesus said about the faith of little children: and be prepared to follow their example and heed their insights. For the kingdom of heaven belongs to such as these.

We would do well also to consider God's love for little children. Not only does Jesus constantly welcome infants and draw lessons for us from their trust and love. He defends them against the brusqueness of adults. When the disciples want to dismiss the children for fear of wasting Christ's time, he intervenes and draws them close. When the Pharisees in the Temple want to stop the children's noisy praises, Jesus refuses to comply, for he delights in their youthful exuberance.

In a more sombre tone Jesus also gives a dire warning to those who violate children. For God honours the vulnerability and dependency of youngsters, and has put them in adult care for nurturing and protection. Yet some children known little nurturing. Some live for years under regimes of fear and anxiety, waiting for the step of a violent parent or step-parent on the stairs, silent with horror at what might come next. Others avoid being home when drunken arguments take place, cautious about what they should say, or how they should look lest it be misinterpreted and generate more hostility. Yet others wake up to terrifying nightmares, fearful because the one they trust is also the one who abuses, and the world is a horribly confusing place. In my own counselling I have met many who have been locked into a guilty silence throughout their child-hood, unable to speak of the secret because who would believe them, and because they feel that they themselves must be the ones who are to blame.

Child abuse goes beyond that which happens in homes, however. We have created an abusing culture, a culture impatient with children for being children, disrespectful to their immaturity, and heedless to their needs. We pump lead into the atmosphere which damages their brain cells, and allow fast cars to make the streets around their homes dangerous and frightening. We create an environment of incessant noise, whether of traffic, loud discos, or personal stereos, which damages the delicate sound mechanisms in their ears and contributes to the ever-rising phenomenon of adolescent deafness. We target them for advertising wherever more useless, peripheral and empty commodities are pushed their way to boost sales and make profits. Only lip service is given to protecting the children in our society from ways of life which are destructive, and then we tut-tut at those youngsters who become hooked on gambling, theft, debt and drugs. Into these situations come the words of Jesus, full of love and care for those who are still in adult charge. His language is powerful; his images are spine-chilling. Warnings which he issues in few other contexts confront us with awful clarity: 'Woe to those who cause any one of these young ones who believe in me to sin. It would be better for that person that a millstone were put around his neck and he were thrown into the sea.'

From these examples we get just a glimpse of the heart of God for children. There is no time in any of our lives when we are too young or too insignificant for God to care about us and for us. This is evident throughout the Scriptures. The Psalmist encounters it when he thinks about his own life. God's presence and involvement have been there from the earliest moments; even in the very act of creation. The psalmist who confessed 'you created my inmost being, and knit me together in my mother's womb' went on to declare:

> I praise you because I am fearfully and wonderfully
>   made;
> your works are wonderful, I know that full well.
> My frame was not hidden from you when I was made
>   in the secret place.
> When I was woven together in the depths of the earth,
> Your eyes saw my unformed body. (*Psalm* 139:15)

When we read this psalm we begin to grasp the way in which God has access to the lives and the hearts of the tiniest infant, and how, in ways we cannot understand, children themselves can make their own response to God. It helps us to see even more the significance of what happened in the story which Luke relates. For Elizabeth has grasped so clearly what was spoken many years before in that psalm. And so the leap for joy of the baby in her womb was nothing more than we might expect. For the creator God is the God who loves the little ones of the creation, and who calls them to praise and adoration. And the coming of the Saviour, disclosed to this unborn infant in the power of the Holy Spirit, was the greatest excuse for a hearty leap and jump that any baby has ever known. The enormous value which God places on the lives of infants and young people is something which he wants us too to respect. May we adults today, into whose care God has entrusted children, learn, like that woman of long ago, to encourage the young ones in our guardianship to grow in faith, trust and worship. And may we adults and children together be able to recognize the love God has given us, and together respond in joy.

Unexpected witnesses to God's Glory

Human beings have through the ages been called to confess and witness to the praise of God. In so many everyday as well as extraordinary places God calls forward people to worship, to declare publicly who God is and draw others into obedience and faith. Yet what this incident reminds us is that witness to God can come unexpectedly from those parts of the creation which we expect to be silent. The baby in the womb has no voice, yet can rejoice in the love and power of God. And this is true everywhere. Not only are the skies themselves chattering day after day about God's glory (Psalm 19:1–3), but the lightning bolts report to God and the eagles soar at his command (Job 38, 39). Every animal of the forest is his, and the cattle on a thousand hills. God knows every bird in the mountains, and all creatures of the field are witnesses to their Creator (Psalm 50). The deserts and fountains, seas and mountains all proclaim that the Lord is God and there is no other.

Our modern societies have tried hard to build cities which give out a different testimony. For much of contemporary society is caught up not in the worship of God, but of self and success, wealth and power. This is reflected in our use of space, our self-indulgence over transport, and our public disregard for those who live in congested or polluted areas. And even what was obviously inspired by God-worship in our cities has become less significant. Beautiful old churches and cathedrals erected to the majesty of God are often physically overshadowed by brash monuments in praise of money and human achievement.

Francis Schaeffer used to tell about an illuminating conversation between a Christian who was a scientist and a man who was an agnostic and very caught up in ideas of the irrelevance of God. As they walked through the streets of New York, dwarfed by skyscrapers, surrounded by traffic noise and jostling crowds, the agnostic warmed to his subject. With scarcely a break for breath he extolled the wonders of human reason, human science, human progress. God was a myth, a useful imaginary concept for a preEnlightened age, but redundant in the face of the modern city. After half an hour his companion suggested they turn into Central Park, and continue the discussion as they watched the ducks and enjoyed the singing of the birds. The trees were beginning to burst out in beautiful spring glory, and proud daffodils stood tall and yellow amidst the new-mown grass. As they laughed at the squirrels chasing each other in flamboyant display, and smelled the sweet fragrances of an April morning, the speaker lost concentration. He started up again as a beautiful white swan glided past with her downy, clumsy cygnets in her wake. Two young romping dogs made him pause next, as, happy and panting, they collided with each other and rolled over down the gentle hill. After a few more tries he stopped, and ruefully admitted, 'It doesn't sound quite so convincing in here.'

When we are surrounded by glorious testimonies to the handiwork of God, it requires an effort of unbelief to deny them. It is a gesture of blind faith to believe that impersonal, random chance is at the centre of the beauty we see, rather than a personal and loving God. That is why people with little contact with church or the creeds can yet find themselves acknowledging the existence and reality of God when they stand on a mountain top, or watch the sun set quietly over the sea. The silent witness of the creation is sometimes so strong that without any warning it has brought people to their knees.

It would be wrong, however, to suggest that the city cannot witness to God. The issue does not involve an ultimate conflict between town and countryside. It involves the question of what we worship. When our culture is bent on worshipping human prowess, it is so much more difficult for people to recognize that they are in the presence of God. Ironically it is also difficult for them to enjoy a high view of human beings. Instead, our cities are also the place of cruelty and violence, of anonymity and deep loneliness. It is when true worship is given to God that it becomes possible for people to be respected for who they really are.

But God can command praise in any context. Even in the harshest or cruellest setting people have suddenly come upon God. For there is nowhere where God has been left without witness. In her moving book *The Hiding Place*, Corrie Ten Boom talks of the witness of God in an ugly and cruel concentration camp. She also tells how God used even humble and irritating fleas as a testimony of divine power. After a few weeks she realized it was they which kept the warders away, and gave her the freedom to open up the love of God for other inmates. In a very real sense the fleas bore witness to the love of God, and through them she was able to give her own prayer of thankfulness!

Luke, the gospel writer, records many other incidents of praise and worship of Jesus, and he never loses the deep awareness that God has put praise and joy into every part of the creation. Towards the end of his record he tells us how exultantly Jesus was worshipped in the city as the crowds threw their cloaks on the road over which he and his donkey were travelling. When the crowd began to go wild with joy, shouting and praising God and recalling the miraculous power they had witnessed, the religious critics told Jesus to keep them quiet. Jesus's response as recorded for us by Luke underlines what has been evident since this very first incident: that God will be praised, and will draw a witness from anything which exists.

'I tell you,' Jesus replied, 'if they keep quiet, the very stones will cry out.'

God has established a powerful witness to his love and truth in the most unanticipated places. The baby in the womb, the goats on the mountains, the stones of the city all leap in joy before the Saviour of the world.

Prayer

I find it so amazing, Lord,
At how you seem to enjoy the praises
Of those whom the world sees as insignificant.
A baby leaps in its mother's womb
Becomes a boogying, praising foetus
And the incident ends up in your Word.
You seem almost absurdly content
When those who have no status,
No privileges
No bargaining power
Choose to give you their little voice.
And become in effect
The wisest of us all.

Questions

1 Can you list some of the characteristics of children that are mentioned in the Bible. How do these compare with the way in which children are seen today?
2 What can we learn, as adults, from the way in which children praise and worship God?

FOUR

GOD'S PROMISES

LUKE 1:45

Blessed is she who has believed that what the Lord has promised to her will come true.

Mary's blessing

When two pregnant women get together it is inevitable that each of them will be excited about her own pregnancy. For even though women show an enormous interest in each other's experience, each one knows how inimicably special is her own growing baby. It is inevitable too that they will try to be fair in their conversation: it would be quite normal to offer mutual congratulations, mutual concern about each other's welfare, and mutual advice.

So there is something not quite normal in the relationship between Mary and Elizabeth. Elizabeth's pregnancy gets very little attention, even though hers is more advanced, and, as an older mother, more risky. Dick France sums it up astutely: 'We do hear words of thanksgiving from each of the two women. But they are not words of *mutual* congratulation: neither has anything to say, directly at least, about Elizabeth and her child. Both concentrate their attention on *Mary's* privilege, and its implications. Even the unborn John adds his gesture of delight at the prospect of Mary's child.'[5]

In a similar way, it is Mary who is described as blessed for believing the promises of God. Yet Elizabeth believed also in what God promised to her. Her own faithfulness is hardly less than that of Mary, for she had to handle a sceptical husband, an incredulous neighbourhood and her own natural doubts. Yet she does not draw attention to herself, either to her forthcoming childbirth, or to her incredible blessing. Her joy is in Mary and in Mary's special news. It is Mary's pregnancy rather than her own which brings out her generous burst of love and rejoicing.

There is more here of course than Elizabeth's modesty, or even than her love for her cousin; more too than the desire to encourage and bless the younger woman. There is a recognition that Mary's pregnancy completely overshadows her own; it fulfils her own. And overjoyed though she is to be giving birth to a child so late in her life, she is yet more overjoyed that Mary is to have a baby. For Mary's son is the long-awaited One, the Promised One of Israel. And the child of Elizabeth has been chosen by God to be the forerunner of his cousin. His life will be spent as the voice in the wilderness who points to the One who comes after. The child of Elizabeth will be the proclaimer-baptizer, announcing to the people 'Behold, your God'. And already, this child and his mother are caught up in the Spirit of God to an awareness of the reality of all that lies ahead. Of course now that the cousins meet Elizabeth does not focus on her own joy, or on her own blessings, for the child that Mary carries is the most significant baby ever born.

Similarly, the generous Elizabeth does not focus on the promises God made to her, or on her own willingness to believe them. She is far more ecstatic because Mary has believed. Mary has believed the promises which have passed through the generation of God's people: that the Redeemer would come; and she has also believed the promises God disclosed specifically to her. And through her belief the word and promise of God was to become the very Word of God incarnate, living among us.

Promises and Belief

There is a strong point being made here. It is that God keeps promises and so it is not foolish to trust this God. And although the promise made to Mary was utterly unique, many people through the ages have believed and trusted that what God has promised will come to pass. The book of Hebrews gives us its own list. Many in the Old Testament believed, in faith, that what God had said, God would accomplish. There was Noah, for example, who believed God about the coming flood, and that his family's obedience would save them from it, and would preserve the animal kingdom from extinction. There was Abraham who believed God's promise about the future, that he and his wife Sarah would be the parents of many nations. And he was prepared to go on believing even when it seemed that God was asking him to sacrifice his only son. There was Moses who believed the promise that God would deliver the people from bondage and slavery. There was Rahab, who believed the promise that she and her family would be kept safe when the walls of Jericho fell. Scripture and history attest to so many who believed and whose faith in God was not in vain.

In our own time there are still many people who risk their lives on the belief that God keeps faith with what he has promised. In many parts of the world Christians make perilous journeys to help each other, trusting God with their welfare and safety. In some areas of the globe the Church continues to teach and preach the Christian Gospel when this is frowned upon or even outlawed by the authorities. Without a deep belief that God is a God who can be trusted, none of this would be possible.

Sometimes, though, people believe God in a very unspectacular and ordinary way. I remember as a child regularly visiting an elderly woman in our church. She was frail, unmarried, cheerful and very active. I called as a matter of routine each month to deliver her parish magazine. It never occurred to me at that time to wonder why she never collected her own parish magazine. She was a more regular worshipper at church than I was, usually managing three services each Sunday. Yet I called at her home as faithfully as I called at the doors of those whose only contact with church was the parish magazine. Over the years my visits grew more frequent, and longer. I would drop round on my way home from school. I would go over to share bits of family or neighbourhood news which she would receive with enthusiasm and sometimes mirth. Her tiny home was always cosy and warming. On a chilly day the heat of her one downstairs room would rise to greet me as I opened the door. The bright red flames of her fire would dart dramatically against the polished black lead stove surrounding. Her kettle hummed out its own welcome, and there would be jam on warm scones. On a summer day the door would be open, the house fragrant with the smell of fresh flowers, picked from her own minute front garden.

She has been dead now for many years, and yet she remains so memorable. Certainly she had her own marked talents: she was the only one among the Sunday School teachers, for example, who could read any passage from the Bible without stumbling over the impossibly difficult names of places or persons. All those men, roll-called from the tribes of Israel in the first chapter of The Book of Numbers, caused her not a pause: Elizur, Shedeur, Shelumiel, the son of Zurishaddai, Amminadab, Isachar, Nethaneel, Zuar, Elishama, Pedahzur, Pagiel, Eliasaph and Amminshadai who begat Ahiezer, trickled off her tongue like any Tom, Dick or Harry. When as an impressed eleven-year-old

I asked her how she did it, she would simply reply with a twinkle, and a cackle: 'Oh, I've read it a few times before.' As well as a knowledge of the Bible she also demonstrated a marked faithfulness to the church. Five minutes before any service began she would be in her seat, quietly preparing herself for worship. She was completely uninterested in issues of church politics, knew nothing, and cared nothing, about the different kinds of churchmanship or 'spirituality', and never entered into any gossip about the local minister. She could be bothered neither with arguing with others nor with judging them. She simply wanted to worship, whatever the weather and whatever the state of her rheumatism.

I remember her most, however, because she was so indefatigably cheerful. She would readily listen to the gripes of others and bring a word of comfort yet seemingly she allowed nothing to get her down. She bore her own growing aches and pains without the need to share them around. 'A trouble shared is a trouble doubled' she used to quip. On one occasion when I was well into my teens she explained to me that the reason for her confident cheerfulness was that she 'believed God's promises'. She was never a text-quoter, yet she would invite me to pick out a little rolled up scroll from the 'promise box', given her by her 'chapel friend'. She would inevitably know the source of the text long before I came to the reference at the end. The central lynchpin of her own life was the promise that whatever happened God would always be with her. It was a full acceptance of St Paul's own testimony at the end of chapter eight in his letter to the Romans. Her version of this read: 'For I am persuaded that neither death nor life nor angels nor principalities nor powers, nor things present, nor things to come, nor height nor depth nor any other creature shall be able to separate us from the love of

God which is in Christ Jesus our Lord' (Romans 8:38 and 39). A promise indeed powerful enough to build a human life on.

Those people who believe that what the Lord has promised will come about, are blessed indeed. And not only do they become enriched in their own person but they enhance the lives of those around them. This was so evidently true of Mary. In the space of a few minutes, Elizabeth was able to experience encouragement, joy and deep fellowship with her cousin. She was able to share the blessings of someone who had believed God; someone who had not reacted in disbelief and fear, but trusted that what God promised would come to be. And that trust reinforced her own faith, and brought her to rejoicing.

Promises and Sorrow

Knowing that there are those who have this kind of faith can for many people be very encouraging. But for others it might be less so. It might bring them a sense of sadness, even despair, that their own faith is so much more fragile and temperamental. For believing that God keeps promises is not always as easy as it sounds. Many Christians find that the disappointments of life are too overwhelming, the sorrows they have had to bear are too heartbreaking. And instead of the simple, believing faith which sees the blessing of God even in the midst of suffering, there is fear and disillusion and cynicism. Belief in the ultimate love of God is still there, yes, but they are now so much more cautious, so much more reluctant to accept that God is a promise-keeper.

It is important therefore to ask what it means to say that God keeps promises. For we can become so excited by the idea that we start to see it as a panacea for all ills. It can end up as a glib and easy phrase to dole out to anyone who is having a difficult struggle. 'Don't worry about anything. God has promised that everything will always turn out right' is not very good advice for someone who is worried to death about a sick child, or a looming redundancy. It can be a very easy way of simply not getting involved with the concerns of the other. Some people have even managed to persuade Christians in the Church that the fact that God keeps promises means that we shall never suffer: we shall never be ill, we shall never have to endure premature bereavement, or depression or loneliness, or unemployment, or betrayal. And it is not only that we *shall* not, but also that we *must* not if we are to be true Christians who take seriously the promises of God. And so those who are bowed down with pain, or devastated with the effects of separation, suffer yet more because they are told they are not experiencing what God has planned for their lives.

This is dangerous theology. It is also wrong. For there is nothing in the Christian faith which encourages us to believe that God's intention is for us to have exactly the kind of life we would like to have. There is nothing in the Word of God which identifies God's promises with a comfortable and pleasant existence, free from any kind of pain, for those who believe them. Instead, suffering is to be expected by every Christian. Suffering comes because we live in a world which is deeply affected by sin and brokenness. Being able to come to terms with this world and with our own barrenness within it can be very difficult. The need just to face their ordinary life is sometimes an arduous and almost unendurable burden for some people. It is impossible to say how many people live with a daily sense of despair, just clinging on, waiting for things to get better. Or people can be filling their lives with activity, keeping going, keeping busy and hoping that in time the pain will decrease. Sometimes of course this works, and we can find new ways of living which can take us away from the intensity, and release us into freedom. And yet for many others nothing improves just by trying to blot it out. Some even have to go through the experience of coming to the very end of everything; to the end of any illusion; to the end of their own hopes and strength. It is as if they have to experience almost a kind of death before there can be new hope and life. Harry Williams writes perceptively of this experience: 'Death is the realistic acceptance of our wilderness for what it is, a refusal to cover it up with simulated experiences of life. Once we accept our wilderness and no longer try to hide it from ourselves, there follows the miracle of resurrection.'[6]

Christians are not exempt from pain and loss and all other effects of a damaged humanity. Christians too suffer pain from the past; they may be familiar with hurt and depression. In fact, other kinds of suffering also will come to us precisely because we believe in God, and therefore reject so many of the values of the world. Far from being a negation of the God who keeps promises to us, the presence of suffering is the very opposite. For the promise of suffering is itself one of the very promises which God makes. 'In the world you will have tribulation,' Jesus tells his closest friends. 'If they persecuted me, they will persecute you also.'

We hear of Christian suffering almost every day of our lives. We hear of those imprisoned, tortured, beaten and rejected because of their faith. I have often felt a sense of solemnity when we say farewell to those who leave the Institute for Contemporary Christianity where I work, or the theological college where I live. I am aware that they may go back to their own countries and face many trials. An Anglican bishop from Uganda and his wife were good friends and neighbours of ours. Their time in London entailed them in separation from their children for over a year, which for each of them was a loss and a source of pain. I would look at the many young smiling faces in the photograph on their table and would always be happy the day they received mail from home, and they found that all was well. When it came time to say goodbye we were sorry to see them go, but happy indeed that they would be where their hearts were, and with those they loved so much. They had been back in a joyful reunion in Uganda for only a short time when the dreadful news leaked through. Their beloved eldest son had been killed in an ambush, meant for the Bishop himself. The depths of grief, remorse, anger and sorrow which they went through can only be guessed at by those of us outside the situation.

Wounding and pain come to so many who respond faithfully to the call of God. Believing what God has promised does not innoculate us against the evil that others would do to us, or against our experience of heartache. It does though bring us into identification with the tragedy and brokenness of humanity. It also brings us into the identification with the sufferings of Christ. It gives us a glimpse of the reality of what St Paul wrote about in his letter to the church at Corinth: 'We are hard-pressed on every side, but not crushed, perplexed, but not in despair, persecuted, but not abandoned, struck down but not destroyed.' Suffering like this makes us realize that the binding up of our deepest brokenness is possible only through the work of God's love. For that love also knew suffering at its deepest level, and was not defeated by it. Those who themselves have gone through great sorrow discover that although many can wound, only God can heal.

People also suffer in other, less dramatic, ways. Sometimes they are humiliated and ridiculed because what they believe is out of step with the group they are part of; some are misunderstood and isolated because they find they have to take stands which separate them from others. 'I was passed over for promotion because I refused to "adjust the books"', explained a Christian friend leaving her first junior accountancy job. 'Now they've found a way of doing without me altogether.'

Every act of suffering affects us in some way or another. With this young woman, the incident matured her as a person. In a small part she too was able to identify with the sorrow of others, and the injustice experienced by many nameless people throughout the world. But it matured her also as a Christian, for she was able to continue the risk of exposing her faith before others. She was able to believe more significantly in the promises of God, and know more deeply what they entailed.

How much then we need to grasp what my elderly friend of decades ago had understood so simply. That the fundamental promise of God is not that we shall not suffer. It is that even though we do suffer, we never do so alone. God is with us in it. For the Incarnation, already in process in the womb of Mary, brings God yet more deeply and directly into the suffering of humanity. Calvin Seerveld sums up the relationship between suffering and the promises of God in his own inimicable way:

Suffering, borne for the sake of showing Jesus Christ's holy, redeeming Rule of love, is a mark of humanity rich with spiritual promises of great blessing (Romans 8:15–18; Philippians 1:27–30; James 1:24; 1 Peter 4:12–16). In fact, for any person who as an adopted child of God in neighbourhooding to others' needs has been stripped of privilege, has been battered back and forth by the competitive professional worlds we inhabit, and who has been and is now left lonely, somewhat humiliated, bypassed by the good people on the way to the temple; the Spirit of the Lord is upon me to promise you relief and protection with our Lord within the genuine body of Jesus Christ. The ashes of mourning on your head are becoming diamonds of a crown, and the depressed spirit that sometimes stifles your joy will be turning into a cloak of laughing halleluiahs.[7]

Mary was to know her own ashes of mourning and perhaps her own confusions about the promises of God. She was to know a stifling of her own joy, as her Son faced the hatred of those who rejected him. Yet her response then was to be as now, one of trust and acceptance. We cannot do any better. We do not understand the purposes of God. We do not know why some of us have to suffer so overwhelmingly. But we can rely on the promise that whatever evil comes our way, there is nothing indeed, in this world or any other, that can separate us from that love which God has poured out for us in Christ Jesus.

The old hymnwriter expressed something of this when he wrote:

God's promise is yea and Amen
And never was forfeited yet.

Prayer

Dear God, I believed your promise
That Christ came to bring us life in abundance.
Which, in my book, means plenty;
Plenty of good work, good times, good friendships,
Plenty of fun, pleasure and peace,
And plenty of life to enjoy them all in.
I really can't see how else 'abundance' can be defined.

So now, dear God, I need to know
Why the lives of so many of your followers
Seem full of poverty, not plenty.
And dogged by suffering, not joy.
Why parents who love their children, suffer painful loss
Why unemployment, hardship, famine, malice, war
Afflict the lives of those you love.

Waiting in the silence, dear God, I have this feeling
That you are not going to give me an answer,
At least, not this side of eternity.
Except perhaps to suggest
That you are well aquainted with our pain
Being involved in it yourself.
And I need to do some more work on definitions.

Questions

1 Why do you think it is difficult to find a modern equivalent to the old word 'blessed'? What are the characteristics about being blessed that Jesus outlines in the Beatitudes (Matthew chapter 5)?

2 What are the areas of suffering in your own life which you have found most difficult, and how real or far away has God seemed to you during these times? How can you pray best when you are hurting?

FIVE

GOD'S GLORY

LUKE 1: 45, 46

And Mary said
'My soul glorifies the Lord.'

Elizabeth's prophetic greeting does more than bless her younger cousin. It releases Mary's tongue into its own song of praise and celebration. For the verses that now follow, the verses we call the Magnificat, are not some carefully crafted poetic soliloquy. They are drawn out of Mary, taking her almost by surprise, as a response to Elizabeth's outburst. What has been revealed to the older woman by the power of the Holy Spirit is now echoed by the younger in a glorious song of spiritual praise and prophetic worship. And she starts where we all must start: by declaring the greatness of God, by glorifying the Lord.

To Glorify God

Yet I wonder how close most people ever come to glorifying the Lord? For we can glorify God only when, like Mary, and in the power of the Holy Spirit, we see a little of God's glory. But the glory of God is not something we can do more than glimpse. It is certainly not something which people in our culture seek after. Even those of us who believe deeply in the love of God, and live our lives in the reality of God's truth, see this glory at best only partially. Dimly, through our sin, and the sins of our society and humanity, we might be sometimes aware of it in a fragmentary way. And although there is evidence of God's glory all around we encounter it only obliquely. We might acknowledge it readily in all the things God has made, in the love God has put within the creation, in God's forgiveness for our sins. Yet when the Bible speaks of the glory, the *shekinah*, it means something deeper than this. It means the very Righteousness of God, the Majesty, the Power, the Splendour, the Light, the Wisdom, the Truthfulness, the Awesome Reality of the Sovereign Creator of all things.

Few human beings have got more than a fleeting glimpse of this. It is a mark of the very mercy of God that we see so little of his Holiness and Splendour. For it would consume us. Our lives would be unable to stand before the overwhelming presence of the glory, the shekinah of God. The Old Testament writers knew this so much better than most of us today. Their sense of awe and reverence before a Creator so mighty made them reluctant even to name the name of God. They could not stand before the majesty of God, but fell on the ground with their faces covered. The people could not come in worship before so holy a Creator without a sacrificial offering for their sins.

When the glory of the Lord was revealed to humans it was often through angelic beings in close contact with God, rather than exposure to God's own self. Even such a revelation produced deep fear. When Daniel received his vision of God's glory his strength failed and his face was drained of all its colour. We read that the impact on those around him was so powerful that although all the other people saw nothing 'a great trembling fell upon them, and they fled and hid themselves.' (Daniel 10:8). The same fear had accompanied the Israelites when Moses came down from Mount Sinai after he had been listening to the voice of God. For the skin of his face shone with reflected light, and the sight was so awesome that his face had to be veiled before the people (Exodus 34:29–35). And in the familiar story of Christ's nativity, the shepherds were visited at

night by the angels, and they fell on the earth in terror for
the 'glory of the Lord shone all around them'.

So God does not quickly invite us into the presence of
the glory. God gives us only as much as we can take when
we seek the Almighty in earnest repentance and humble
faith. But just a momentary glimpse of God's glory is
enough to bring any one of us to humility and worship and
wonder. For then everything else suddenly takes on a new
perspective. We see our own selves with much less delusion. We are shown something of the holiness of God
alongside our petty and tainted lives. We want to release
our souls in praise. We want to be emptied before him in
wonder and adoration, and filled again with his grace and
truth. We have that sense of amazement, as more than one
writer has written, that though God is everything, and I am
nothing, yet God wants me to draw close in love.

And once brought to that place we find ourselves in
fellowship and communion with those who have glimpsed
the glory and praised God before us. For long before we in
the twentieth century wrote our hymns and songs and cho-
ruses of exaltation, people had been making their own
responses with music and art and proclamation. So much
that is important in our lives has at some time been
expressed by song. The experience of joy, elation, love,
sorrow all have flowed over into music and poetry. Exquisite sounds which speak to us at the depth of our being
bring us into a reality which is more than verbal. Carefully
crafted metaphors which take ordinary human words and
chisel them into works of art remind us that we live in a
universe of great possibilities. The provisions of words and
music: of notes, similes, cadences and images, are wonderful gifts from a playful God. They are gifts which draw us
closer and deepen our faith. And these gifts have been used
through the ages to express people's most profound beliefs.

So many stories are told of how the sense of the deep reality of God's greatness has brought from musicians the most exquisite and awe-inspiring music. We remember how the composer Handel was given an overwhelming awareness of the majesty and compassion of God during those few days in which he wrote the whole of *The Messiah*. And centuries before that those women and men in the Old Testament Scriptures were themselves overcome by worship, letting their pens flow freely with the joy of praise and thanksgiving; knowing in their heart what the creation revealed.

The Magnificat

So when Mary lifted up her voice and said 'my soul glorifies the Lord' (or 'my soul declares the greatness of the Lord'), she was testifying to what she too had glimpsed of the transcendent power of God. In singing out her love and worship Mary is therefore continuing that long tradition of faithful servants of God who before her had glimpsed just a little of the *shekinah*.

In this passage we call the Magnificat, Luke records from Mary's mouth the timeless themes of the majesty of God. He brings out a song about the mercy and compassion of the Most High; a song which recalls the glory, the power and the faithfulness of Almighty God. Nothing Mary says here is new. For the words, phrases, sentences which go up to make the Magnificat had already been used time and time again by the people of Israel. She now brings them together in prophetic homage to the God who has so specially blessed her. These themes are indeed her heritage, for they belong to her people. 'Mary is linked with Israel, personified as the daughter of Sion. She springs from the

Jewish people, bears the seeds of the Old Testament and the flowers of the New... She is the woman tied to God's land, linked physically, spiritually, psychologically with her own people.'[8]

Mary, as we have seen, is in every sense a woman rooted in the Jewish faith, and in touch with the teachings which were the legacy of her people. She is a spiritual descendant of those women in the Bible who, before Mary, have sung out in thanksgiving and praise to God. Miriam the prophet, and sister to Moses and Aaron sang and accompanied herself on the tambourine, rejoicing in God's deliverance at the Red Sea. Deborah, the Judge, sang, praising God for their rescue and the peace which was now to come upon Israel for forty years. Hannah sang too as she left her precious son Samuel to serve and minister in the Temple, a song in many ways like that of Mary's own (1 Samuel 2:1–11).

Not just Mary's first cry of exaltation but the whole of what we call the Magnificat is a song of unbridled praise to God's glory. More than almost any other song in the Bible it has linked worshippers across the millennia, in an affirmation of the God before whom human beings of every age and continent together bow in awe.

Even though there is every indication that the song did not originate with Mary, the words are nevertheless so obviously relevant to her own experiences. But neither does the song end with Mary, for in churches and denominations throughout the world, the Magnificat is read, said or sung today as people's own offering of thanksgiving to God. Whether it is encountered as someone probes the gospel of Luke for the very first time, or is encountered as someone sings it for the thousandth time in a new setting at worship, the words still invite us to glory in the Lord. In Anglican churches in particular, those who through the generations have gathered together for evensong have repeated so often the words which Luke has passed down to us.

Yet there is one small observation which perhaps needs to be made. Sometimes in their very familiarity the opening words of Mary's song may have misled us. With some people the old translation 'my soul magnifies the Lord' is much treasured, all the more so because the very words themselves provide such a powerful link with the past, and provide a solemnity of worship which they appreciate. Yet within our contemporary context this phrase might give out the wrong meaning. For we need to understand what it means to magnify God. It is not the same as putting God under a magnifying glass to make God bigger. Mary's praises were not enlarging God. She was not trying to make God greater, more magnificent, more glorious. No human being can do that. She was simply testifying to the glory and greatness which is already there in God, and of which she had glimpsed just a little. In the story that Luke tells Mary was only too aware of her own humility and need of grace. She was under no delusions that she had anything to offer to God's glory and power. Instead, this woman of obedient trust was pouring out her soul in tribute and adoration before the King of Kings and Lord of Lords. She was adding her own voice to the testimony of praise which had gone on since the beginning of time. And whatever words we use, and in whatever context we use them, we too can do nothing more. We can only acknowledge with our hearts and souls that all glory belongs to God.

Mary is given her song to share with us the praises of God; to make the reality of God present in our own lives, to live with the love of God echoing from our lips.

The Prompting of the Holy Spirit

Although the words were written down by Luke, the inspiration for them came from the very God that Mary was praising, from the same God who had inspired his faithful people throughout the ages. They witness to the powerful truth that the God who revealed his glory to Moses was the same God who would deliver the Messiah through Mary. Mary's song is a powerful gift of the Holy Spirit. But the Holy Spirit was active long before Mary's outpouring of joy. And as well as those women we have already mentioned, there were many others in the Scriptures who had known in their own soul the Spirit's inspiration and uplifting. We recall Moses centuries earlier when he too sang out in praise of God, as is recorded in the book of Exodus (15:1–3):

> The Lord is my strength and my song; he has become
> my salvation.
> He is my God and I will praise him, my father's God
>   and I will exalt him

and the refrain was continued in Miriam's own inspired song:

> Praise to the Lord for he is highly exalted. (*verses* 20, 21)

In 2 Samuel 22:47 David shouted:

> The Lord lives and
> Blessed be my Rock!
> May the God of my salvation be exalted.

The Holy Spirit's testimony to God's power and greatness is there throughout the Bible. In the psalms particularly we are given a deep sense of God's glory: sometimes in song and dancing, sometimes in profound affirmations of the uniqueness of God. Asaph, one of the psalmists, touched into the deepest truths of life when he asked:

> Whom have I in heaven but you, and earth has nothing
> I desire beside you.
> My flesh and my heart may fail,
> but God is the strength of my heart and my portion for
> ever. (*Psalm* 73:25)

Other psalms are given over wholly to declaring and inviting others to God's praise.

> Praise the Lord from the Heavens praise him in the
> heights above.
> Praise him all his angels,
> praise him all his heavenly hosts,
> praise him sun and moon,
> praise him all you shining stars. (*Psalm* 148)
> Sing to the Lord a new song,
> his praise in the assembly of the saints. (*Psalm* 149)

Not only the psalmists but the prophets also were caught up in the Spirit to catch a picture of the glory and power of the God of all creation. Isaiah urged his hearers:

> Sing to the Lord, for he has done glorious things.
> Shout aloud and sing for joy, people of Zion,
> for great is the Holy One of Israel among you. (*Isaiah* 12:5–6)

Through the Spirit the prophet Jeremiah declared:

No one is like you, O Lord, You are great, and your
name is mighty in power.
Who should not revere you, O King of the nations?
This is your due. (*Jeremiah* 10:6, 7).

And Habakkuk had his own vision of God's magnificence
and power:

His glory covered the heaven
And his praise filled the earth.
His splendour was like the sunshine,
Rays flashed from his hand.

Throughout the Old Testament the Holy Spirit is constantly revealing something of God's majesty and splendour. But
whereas there this majesty is always at a great distance, in
the New Testament it is brought closer. For the gospel of
John tells us that the glory of God became incarnated in
bodily form.

The Word was made flesh and dwelt among us.
We have seen his glory, the glory of the Only Begotten
One
who came from the Father, full of grace and truth.

Jesus Christ, the Word, the Lamb of God, the Messiah, the
Saviour of the World, is the image of the Invisible God. In
Christ all the glory of God has been made apparent. And
Mary's cry 'My Soul glorifies the Lord' was prophetic
indeed, for the Lord of glory had already taken up resi-
dence with her.

In the very last book of the New Testament, the Book of Revelation, the apostle John draws together so many of the testimonies to the all-consuming Truth and Splendour of God. In one powerful vision he witnesses the utter brilliance of the Creator-Redeemer. John describes what he saw in the City of God:

> I saw no temple in the city, for its temple is the Lord God Almighty and the Lamb. And the city has no need of sun or moon to shine upon it, for the glory of God is its light and its lamp is the Lamb. The nations will walk by its light and the kings of the earth will bring their glory into it. Its gates will never be shut by day – and there will be no night there.

The Holy Spirit not only gives the vision of God's glory to those who receive it, but through them shares it with us. The pictures are graphic, the words imageric and exciting, the language dramatic and colourful. And although clumsy human speech can never be adequate to describe the reality of Utterly Perfect Being, we are given some indication, some sense, of God's supremacy and glorious majesty.

There will always be a mystery about how God communicates with us. For the words are human words, penned or spoken by human authors, with different temperaments and styles of expression, yet the inspiration is of the Holy Spirit. The men and women story-tellers describe what they know in vivid images written down in specific cultures, yet the Holy Spirit directs them and applies them to our hearts today. This same mystery lies behind how we should communicate with God. For although our praising and our praying comes from us, we know that the direction should come from the Holy Spirit. We struggle to find the words we want yet it is God the Holy Spirit who teaches each of us how to worship, and what to say in the presence of God. We feel inarticulate and inadequate, bewildered how to tell God all we want to say. Yet it is the Holy Spirit who takes our feeble efforts and lifts them into praise to the Godhead. There is so much we do not know about how the Spirit can help us in praising God. As the apostle Paul says in his letter to the church in Rome, we do not even know how to pray as we ought. But the Holy Spirit intercedes for us with prayers too deep for words.

There is one other point about the Holy Spirit which is important here. The Spirit is changing us so that we are more able to experience God's majesty and splendour. For because Jesus himself is the very glory of God, those who love Christ reflect more and more of God's glory when the Holy Spirit works in their lives. In explaining this to the young Corinthian church the apostle Paul referred back to the way Moses needed to veil his face because he had been in contact with God's glory. But Jesus has brought that splendour so much closer, and even allows us to come into deeper experience of it: 'we, who with unveiled faces all reflect the Lord's glory, are being transformed into his like-ness with ever-increasing glory which comes from the Lord, who is the Spirit' (2 Corinthians 3:7–18). Because of Jesus the Holy Spirit leads us with freedom to come into the very presence of God, to worship, to praise and to glimpse more and more of the glory of the Almighty Redeemer.

These are indeed truths which it is hard for many of us to grasp. Sometimes we understand them in our experience before we can appreciate them with our minds. But we need time to grasp some of the deep truths about the glory of God and how to praise through the Spirit of God. Often, it is only when we are prepared to spend more of our time in readiness before our Redeemer that we begin to understand what it really means to worship; only when we take time out of the rush of life to be quiet before the Creator of all things that we discover more about the power of the Holy Spirit in our own lives; only when we care more about God's majesty than our own convenience that we begin to get some glimpse of the infinite greatness and holiness of God.

Mary's own simple gesture of worship and thankfulness indicates that her trusting soul knows already how to glorify and praise the Lord. As we join her response of obedience in our own words and song, may we too be drawn into a greater vision of what it means to magnify the God of glory.

Prayer
Creator God
Whose glory fills the heavens
And the earth
And the vast horizons we see from our aeroplanes
And the planets and stars visible through our radio telescopes
And the depths of the oceans plumbed by our submarines
And the arctic wastes filmed for us confident explorers.
And the silent mountain pinnacles climbed by the few and fit.
And the eagle on her nest, and the woodpecker's crest,
And the thick peat bogs, and the toads and the frogs,
And the antelope, the ant, the wildebeest, the elephant,
And salmon come to spawn, the colours of the dawn,
And the atom, the ion, the quark, and the prion.
And everything else,
Thank you for showing us
Only so much of your glory
As we can bear.

Questions

1 Mary could talk about God's glory more easily than we can now because it was so much part of her history and culture. What kinds of things today help you to understand the glory of God?

2 How would you put into your own words what the apostle John means about Jesus when he says 'we have seen his glory, the glory of the one and only Son who came from the Father'?

SIX

GOD'S SALVATION

LUKE 1:47

My spirit rejoices in God my Saviour.

Many people have more than an inkling about what Mary meant when she said that her spirit rejoiced. Some of the most sublime experiences in worship have been experiences of rejoicing. They can come when together in the Church we have declared the greatness of God. We ponder and reflect on the magnificence and holiness of the Creator, and suddenly, often without warning, find ourselves filled with deep joy. There is joy at the sheer beauty of the creation: the swallows that swoop and play before getting down to the serious business of nest-building and rearing their young; the gladioli that burst uninvited and uncoaxed into a blaze of colour. There is joy too in the very reality of God. The cosmic becomes personal; the far-off becomes face-to-face. This same Majestic Creator who guides the swallows and unfolds the buds is also our own Saviour and Redeemer. We stand, without even having been aware of it, in the presence of Love. And our sense of awe and amazement is transformed to one of awe and rejoicing. C.S. Lewis summed this up so well when he talked of his own journey, from atheism to theism, then from theism to Christianity. He was, as in the title of his book, *Surprised by Joy*.

The joy is not merely human joy. In the biblical narrative it is experienced also by many different parts of creation. Isaiah tells us that even the desert will be caught up in expressing it:

> The desert and the dry-lands will exult,
> The wilderness will rejoice and blossom,

Like the crocus, it will burst into bloom,
It will rejoice greatly and shout for joy. (*Isaiah* 35:1)

It is a wonderful picture of over-the-top, exuberant abandon. It is the parched world bursting into verdant glory and joining its voice with those of human beings. Together with thick green leaves and bright pink blossom, fat spring caterpillars and nesting birds, we are caught up in joy before the presence of God.

Happiness and Joy

I can imagine that some people might find this picture a little overdone. Some might even feel completely outside it. One of the reasons for that is that joy is not a characteristic our society knows much about. In fact joy, real joy, is in short supply in our world today.

This may sound odd when we reflect on how very much people want to be happy. So much money, energy, time and trouble is committed to the pursuit of happiness. 'I don't mind what she does, just as long as she is content', sighs an anxious mother. 'I know his wife wouldn't like our relationship, but I can make him happy', argues a woman on the edge of an affair with a married colleague. Our need for happiness has almost become a religious pursuit. Wherever we go in the West we are surrounded by hoardings urging us to buy more and more commodities which will ensure that we have a good life. If we drive this car we will be happy; if we drink this beer, sleep on this bed, travel with this agency, eat this breakfast cereal, wash our hair with this shampoo, and install this gas fire, we will be blissfully content. This pizza parlour will make our grumbling children congenial; this expensive car will make our nasty divorce pleasant.

Of course, nobody believes it.

Even young people learn that happiness is seldom bought, and even when it is the effects are transient. Because this thing we call happiness depends so much on being with the right people, in the right situation, with the right things around us. And people can find that even after a lifetime's search it still eludes them. A colleague of mine was talking to a man who had messed up so much of his life. He had always required a substantial income because he spent heavily on entertainment and clothes. After years of an unhappy marriage, he had finally left his wife to move in with a lover. This relationship was short-lived and after a few months the lover decided to move out. His firm had noted for some time his poor performance at work, and he was the first to go in a round of redundancies. Bouts of heavy drinking followed, and a careless decision during a hangover could have had disastrous consequences at his next job, which he consequently lost within a month. A year later he was unemployed, and deeply in debt. Six months after that his flat was repossessed. His sister eventually lost sympathy as he constantly landed on her family for meals and accommodation, irrespective of their own needs. When in desperation he talked to my colleague he couldn't understand why life had been so hard on him. 'I never asked for very much,' he insisted, 'I only ever wanted to be happy.'

The problem is that happiness is not something we can chase after. We cannot command it to appear at our whim. When we do, we find so often that it eludes us. I know many people who dread birthdays, or anniversaries, or big events because they hate being let down. They want to create something significant on these occasions, something that is especially happy, and that they can look back on for years to come. Yet, all too often the event does not live up to the expectation, and disappointment sets in. Others find that the pressures of life crowd out any possibility of happiness. 'Happy?' repeated one man incredulously to an interviewer's question, 'Only when I'm drunk.' And we probably all know people who are happy only when they are miserable. The reality is that as they get older most people's lives are not particularly happy ones. There is so much in our adult world which reminds us of sorrow or heartache. Some people's lives are full of quite deep *un*happiness; grief and regret are for them far too frequent companions.

So it can be reassuring to realize that the Christian faith does not put that much store on happiness. For even if it comes, it is at best simply a by-product of living lives that are meaningful and content, and seeking the best for others. That is why it is not one of the characteristics Christians are asked to aim for. St Paul did not write about 'love, happiness, peace' when he talked of the fruit of the Spirit. He wrote about *joy*. And joy is not situational. It does not depend on everything being the way I want it. It is not something I must seek desperately in case it eludes me again. Joy is something deeper, more abiding, less fragile. As a hitchhiker explained: 'Happiness is finding a wallet full of $20 notes with no identification in it. Joy could hit you as you give your last $5 to a lovable rogue with an unlikely story. Happiness is the preserve of the lucky, the wealthy and the successful. Joy belongs to any who find it, and the poor seem to find more of it than most.'[9]

Joy, then, is never self-centred or self-congratulatory. Instead it involves recognizing that the needs of others are at least equal to those of our own. It is possible to know joy even when we are grieving. To keep on rejoicing does not mean walking about with a toothpaste-advertising smile fixed on our faces. It means experiencing our humanity in the context of hope and love. Mike Riddell tells his guitar-strumming readers: 'Joy is when your heart picks up the vibrations of God and for a brief time beats in harmony; when your love echoes God's love; when your gift resonates with God's.'[10] Joy is something that keeps us 'on track', because it comes when we know God's values for our lives, and live with trust and playfulness in God's love and compassion. That's why the Apostle could write to the Thessalonians telling them to 'Rejoice always, pray continually, in everything give thanks' even in the midst of persecution.

It is joy, then, that Mary sings of in her outburst of praise. Of course, Mary may well also have been very happy. There was a lot to be happy about. She was with her beloved cousin, and they were both pregnant and excited. She was at the end of an arduous journey, and it was going to be good to sit down, and catch up on masses of family news. With newly baked bread on the table, a pot of good food and carefully made gifts to exchange, I can imagine that a whole evening of enjoyment and relaxation would celebrate the family reunion. But what flows between the cousins is more than happiness. What is released in Mary's outburst is the overflowing of *joyful* exuberant fullness, a freedom of spirit which is overwhelmed with God's goodness. It is a joy that will stay with her through hardship and sorrow; it is a joy that will persist even when her heart is pierced with pain. For at its root it is not founded on swings of human mood or on circumstance. Her joy is rooted in God her Saviour.

God and Salvation

To rejoice in the salvation of God was something which the Jewish tradition would have taught Mary from an early age. The concept of Saviour was a strongly Messianic concept. From the earliest books of the Bible the people of Israel had praised God and given thanks for their deliverance.

In the biblical text of the Old Testament salvation was almost always associated with rescue or deliverance. Mary would know the many stories about the way the Israelites had regularly been rescued from the hands of their enemies. She would know the many forms of jeopardy that had confronted them. God was praised for coming to their aid in every situation: for saving them from slavery and oppression in Egypt (Exodus 15:2), for redeeming their lives from the pit (Psalm 103:4), for saving Jonah from the belly of the fish (Jonah 2:9), for saving the needy from death (Psalm 72:13). For the people of Israel the Saviour God was also the Protector God, both delivering the people and keeping them safe. Mary would be familiar with the way this is expressed in many images in the Old Testament. There, God is a Rock (Deuteronomy 32:4), a Fortress (2 Samuel 22:2), a strong Tower into which the righteous can run and be safe (Proverbs 18:10).

Yet salvation became associated with deliverance not just from physical evil, but also from spiritual and moral evil. God was the one who through the call of the prophets called the people to repentance and offered them redemption. God was the one who through the sacrifices of the priests forgave the wrongs of the people and showed mercy. God was the one who through the kings enacted justice and ruled with fairness. And when the kings or the priests were corrupt the whole people would suffer.

This salvation power of God was unique. It was shared by none of the gods of the neighbouring peoples. When God spoke to the people through the prophet Isaiah we read a dramatic proclamation of this uniqueness. The claim is clear: God alone is the righteous God and Saviour.

I am the Lord and there is no other.
I have not spoken in secret
From somewhere in a land of darkness ...
Ignorant are those who carry about idols of wood,
And pray to gods who cannot save ...
There is no God apart from me,
a righteous God and a Saviour,
there is none but me.
Turn to me and be saved,
all you ends of the earth;
for I am God and there is no other. (*Isaiah* 45:18–22)

There is so much then in Mary's religious tradition that
would have given her a deep understanding of salvation. It
involves deliverance and rescue at so many levels, and it
comes from God alone.

Yet she knew also that God's salvation was not complete. The full redemption which had been promised,
and anticipated in so many of the Jewish rituals and cele-
brations, had not yet been fulfilled. The hope of the people
of Israel was for the Christ of God, the Messiah who was
to come as Saviour and Redeemer. That Messiah was the
one for whom they watched and waited, the one who, in
the words of the writer to the Hebrews, was to be Prophet,
Priest and King.

Mary's rejoicing in God her Saviour is therefore full of
deep significance. For she is both rejoicing in the salvation
of God which the people of Israel had known from the very
beginning, and in the very Messianic hope that the Christ
will come. Yet even as she rejoices the hope is being fulfilled in the child which is growing within her. Her Saviour
now takes on humanity and when the time is due he will be
born as the prophets foretold.

Mary's Saviour

It is also significant that Mary refers to the Redeeming God as *her* Saviour. Luke takes the Old Testament title for God and makes it personal to Mary. Mary, like all those before her, sings of her own deliverance, identified with that of the whole people of God. In using this form, Mary is not confessing any personal sin here. She is simply adding her voice to those that have gone before, and counting herself amongst the delivered ones. God must be her Saviour before she can offer him to others.

Nevertheless, there is nothing in Mary's song, or indeed in the rest of the gospels, which suggests that the other dimension of salvation is not also applicable to Mary. There is everything to indicate that Mary's Son becomes also her Saviour, as much as he becomes the Saviour of the rest of the world. For in our concern to honour Mary as the mother of the Lord, we must also see how much she comes to us as an ordinary, believing woman. In the writings of Matthew, Mark, Luke and John, Mary is presented to us in so many situations. We see her, anxious and clumsily impatient when her twelve-year-old son is missing from the travelling party after their trip to Jerusalem. We see her, full of perceptiveness at the marriage of Canaan, when she persuades Jesus to produce a miraculous supply of wine and so save the face of the host. We see her with her other children, possessively wanting attention from Jesus, trying to distract him from his teaching and healing, and receiving instead a rebuff. We hear a woman in the crowd attempting to adulate Christ's mother shouting, 'Blessed is the womb that bore you and the breasts that you sucked.' And we hear Jesus's reply, discouraging such adulation: 'Blessed rather are those who receive the word of God and obey it.' There is no suggestion in the biblical account that Mary is perfect before God or without any kind of sin. In each of the four gospels Mary is presented as a woman who is in many respects very much like one of us. We can agree wholeheartedly with the Jesuit commentator on Luke who describes Mary as 'the first representative of faith in his account, *vis-à-vis* all those who will accept her Son in faith'.[11]

And so in this song of rejoicing, Mary is acknowledging personally that Yahwe is the Saviour of the world. In humbling herself before God she is aware of her own need and dependence upon God. And as the time comes for her to be delivered of this child she will need the over-seeing and protection of Yahwe in a very special way. For the rest of her life she will have to learn to be patient, and to let go of her anxiety. During her Son's infant years she will need to learn to trust God for his safety and well-being; during his young adulthood she will need to stand aside and allow him to leave the family trade for a greater work. She will have to leave off her maternal demands, and accept the fact that he will not put her before the greater needs of others. She will have to stand by as he is mistreated and suffers injustice. She will have to endure the devastating grief of having to watch him die a horrible death. And as old Simeon in the Temple is later to prophesy, a sword will indeed pierce her own heart. She may even have to struggle with the question of the meaning of it all, or whether God could really have intended all this grief and heartache. Mary will need to bring before God whatever fears, or pain, lack of trust, or shortcomings invade her life and her heart. There can be no doubt that the coming Christ, who will die on a criminal's gallows outside the walls of the city, is to be Mary's Redeemer, and that of all other human beings who call upon him.

Nor, of course, does Mary claim otherwise. For in everything she says and does she shows a deep awareness of her own humility. She is very alert to her human inadequacy, and so pours out her gratitude for God's abundant love and care. This is what her song is all about. Mary does not draw our attention to herself. She does not ask us to exalt her. She points us instead to the deliverance of Yahwe, and anticipates the coming of the Christ, the Saviour and Redeemer of the world.

Prayer
Christ, the redeeming one,
Saviour of the world.
I am so grateful
That the world
Includes me.

Questions
1 Describe how you see the difference between joy and happiness. What does St Paul mean when he calls joy one of the 'fruits of the Spirit'?
2 If we believe that God is our Saviour, what do we need to be saved from?

SEVEN

GOD'S CHOOSING

LUKE 1:48

For he has been mindful of the humble state of his servant
From now on all generations shall call me blessed.

For centuries people have been chosen for certain tasks on
the basis of fairly strict criteria. Kings and queens inherited
their titles from relatives, with the odd bit of bloodshed and
insurrection thrown in for testing. Musicians were appointed because of their talents and musical dexterity (although
they might lose a finger for a wrong note). Teachers were
chosen because of their accumulated wisdom or scholarly
ability (although if they fell out of favour they could, like
Socrates, end up drinking hemlock). Long before our twen-
tieth-century ideas of 'meritocracy' (ideas of course not
always put into practice), people made sure that those they
chose for important jobs had either skill or status.

   This can be seen today too in many obvious and practi-
cal ways. If we want to find an architect who will draw
plans for an extension for our house, we require professional qualifications. We don't take on the man who
arrives at our door simply because he dresses well, and can
do nice thumbnail sketches. We want to see some evidence,
to make sure in advance that the plans he draws won't
make our home look like the House that Jack Built. Or if
we want to appoint a doctor to a consultancy in traumatic
surgery we won't take on someone merely because she
looks good in her white overall and can handle knives very
well. We shall want to be assured that the person in front
of us is a qualified, established surgeon and not a junior
butcher or part of a circus act.

   If then we are so discriminating in the persons we
appoint, how much more might we expect God to be?

How carefully God needs to look at our credentials when what is at stake is not just people's health or homes, but their eternal lives. And certainly, when within the Church we look for those who will serve God most effectively we want to make sure that they are people of integrity, of wisdom, of prayer, of spiritual leadership. We like it too if they have some education, have a good reputation in the community, are good decision-makers and administrators and can handle people well.

Yet, as Mary now reminds us, it sometimes seems that God's way of choosing is less discriminating than our own. God doesn't even seem to shortlist the most suitable candidates and take up references. For the job of mother to the coming Redeemer, God chooses someone whom history, and we ourselves, would surely have otherwise utterly overlooked. Mary, gentle, pleasant and warm though she may well have been, had no status, no credentials, no qualifications. From a human perspective she was a nobody. As one writer puts it: 'It is typical of God, who delights to reverse the world's ideas of importance, that he has taken notice of an insignificant servant girl.'[12]

Many people go to great lengths to try to explain to us why God chooses those whom he uses. (Others of course go to great lengths to tell us why God may not choose certain groups of people for his work.) I am going to make no such attempt. That is nothing to do with any personal modesty – it is because I simply do not know. The reasons behind God's sovereign choices are understood by God alone. They are part of the mystery of our faith. What we do know is that God's choice is often a long way from what ours might be. This was illustrated in the Old Testament by God's choice of another significant figure, David. When God sent the faithful prophet Samuel to choose a new king for Israel, Samuel left to himself would have picked the wrong person. He was far too quickly taken in by an impressive physique and height. God had to explain then, what many have been reminded of since: 'Human beings look on the outward appearance, but the Lord looks at the heart' (1 Samuel 16:7). Seven candidates later, Samuel understood what God meant.

Outward Appearances

This human habit of judging one another on the basis of appearances has many times been our downfall. Yet there are many reasons why we do it. Sometimes it is because we do not have much else to go on. We have so few criteria of how to assess people that we make the wrong assessment. It can leave us literally destitute. Many have been left at the mercy of unscrupulous people who exploit our readiness to trust what they say, or our keenness for a bargain. The rising tide of fraud gives witness to how easy it is for people to see only what others want them to see: the affable, 'sincere', businessman demeanour masking the ruthless charlatan, who is unconcerned about fair dealings, or the hardship of those he cheats. Or there are people who have gone into marriage or close relationships because they have been taken in by appearances. They have had little real knowledge of the other person's character, and the result has brought great suffering. 'I had no idea when I married him that he was a violent man', one wife told me after a decade of physical cruelty. 'I had no idea she would always treat me with such contempt', confessed a man whose wife had demoralized him publicly and in private for over five years. And there are stories of so many others who commit their lives to people who turn out to be habitually unfaithful, unable to sustain a relationship of committed marital intimacy.

But if outward appearances let us down when we *try* to make careful judgements about people, how much more dangerous are they when we don't? Sometimes we deliberately focus upon exteriors. We allow ourselves to get caught up with the externals of people's lives and status. In fact, it is odd that so many people become personally interested in the lives of the famous. For the cult of personalities has been thoroughly thrust upon us. We can read about the important, the notorious, the rich, the Royals, the media stars any day of our lives. We can find out what they had for breakfast. We can read all about their extramarital affairs. We can debate whether they might have bulimia, or cancer or AIDS. We can listen in to their taped phone calls, for a charge of 45p a unit. Some newspaper reporters kindly spend days and nights outside their homes for us, documenting who comes in and who goes out, photographing what goes on in the garden, the dining room and even the bedroom if the curtains are left open. Thousands of column inches are spent speculating about the relationships of television personalities. Whole pages are devoted to the jetsetting of the soap opera actors. And when the parts they play become more interesting than real life, then who cares if the two become merged, the realities completely blurred, and there is nothing left other than appearances.

The trouble is, we often operate according to similar criteria in our own lives. We allow ourselves to become impressed by the high standing or repute of others. We are dazzled by their success, their importance or their opulence. And as a result we defer to them, judging them to be of greater worth and value than those who impress us less. We are pleased if we are included in their circle. We are delighted if we can drop their name nonchalantly into a conversation. Some of us go out of our way to cultivate *useful* relationships; manoeuvring invitations to make sure we associate with those we aspire to be like. We show favouritism to those who might do us some good. We flatter the influential in the hope that these people will find us congenial and remember us at the right moment. And all the time what matters are the outward appearances: influence, possessions, promotion, hand-outs, being in the right group. The sad thing is that there is often a high price to pay for membership.

The apostle James talks about these attitudes in his letter. He is rudely down-to-earth in his advice to the Church: 'Don't show favouritism. Suppose a man comes into your meetings wearing a gold ring and fine clothes, and a poor man in shabby clothes comes in. If you show special attention to the man wearing fine clothes and say, "Here's a good seat for you", but say to the poor man, "You stand there", or "You sit on the floor by my feet", have you not discriminated among yourselves and become judges with evil thoughts?' James is simply passing on the warning which God gave to the prophet Samuel many years before.

It sounds so obvious, and yet looking down the centuries it is advice which the Church itself has been reluctant to take. Even though it is now not so blatantly related to gold rings and fine clothes, there are still patterns of discrimination in our churches, patterns of associating with those who matter, and ignoring or patronizing those who do not. People are often voted in to eldership or councils because of the influence they can wield elsewhere. Sometimes we see the problem reflected in the very issue that James raised: where people sit!

I well remember an incident related to me some years ago. An Anglican church in a semi-rural area was facing falling electoral roles and struggling to keep its incumbent. A new young vicar was appointed to try to get the church back on its feet, and among many other things he was excited about the possibility of mission. After almost a year's planning and praying, a team of people came to help the churchgoers to spread the Good News through the parish, and invite more people along. On the second evening meeting they were rewarded by a good handful of new people in the church. As they waited in the still half-empty building for the worship to begin, a longstanding member of the congregation and church council walked over to where one of the newcomers was sitting. He tapped her smartly on the shoulder. 'Excuse me,' he said, 'that's the chairman's seat.'

I have it on good authority that the issue about who should sit where occupies a great deal of time and energy in some of our churches and cathedrals. It has become enshrined in a ritualistic protocol. Where to process and in what order, who walks with whom, and who walks alone, are all closely guarded privileges which are rehearsed at the beginning of every important induction or enthronement. What is all too evident to anyone watching, is that there is still an elaborate pecking order, where the ecclesiastically distinguished and the ordained hierarchy take inevitable preference over the *ordinary* laity. Status is reinforced by clerical dress: the colour of robes, the wearing of mitres, marking out the various rungs of the hierarchy. It not only feels quaintly archaic, but the whole procedure seems oblivious to the central point which both James and Samuel warned us against. It seems even more odd when it is at the centre of *Christian* worship.

Of No Reputation

God, however, had no pecking order when the birth of Christ was organized. He was uninterested in both worldly status or in the status of those who had made a name for themselves in the religious hierarchy. When God wanted to choose someone for this great calling it was neither in the king's palace, nor in the Temple that the search was mounted. Instead, Mary was the one picked out; an ordinary humble woman who came from Bethlehem. No wonder she sang in amazement and gratitude 'he has been mindful of the humble state of his servant' (reflecting also Hannah's prayer in the first book of Samuel, chapter one). God noticed Mary, in spite of her lack of status. What was God looking for in such a person? We do not know. We do not know whether there was anything specifically about Mary herself that was important. All we can be sure of is that God applied his own criterion already given to Samuel: that whereas we look on the outward appearance God looks on the heart. In the heart of Mary, God saw someone who would respond in faith and love. In that heart was the willingness to trust, and the openness of prayer.

But Mary's lack of status remains significant. Because of course it was also going to reflect on her Son. In coming to live among us as the son of a carpenter's wife, Jesus was accepting Mary's humble position as his own. He would have few influential friends in Herod's court, or amongst the High Priestly group. He would have no easy access to the Roman Governor or be able to rely on support in high places. Whatever income he required he would have to earn, or accept independence from his friends. Whatever home or belongings he needed would be found in humble surroundings. He would live among ordinary people and be subject to the same hardships as they. And as he told his would-be followers, sometimes he would live with deprivations. 'Foxes have holes,' he said, 'and the birds of the air have nests. But the Son of man has nowhere to lay his head.' The apostle Paul sums up this servant status and its implications. He says we should be like Jesus:

> who being in very nature God,
> did not consider equality with God something to be
>   grasped,
> but made himself nothing,
> taking the very nature of a servant. (*Philippians* 2:6, 7)

There is then a great deal which we do not know about God's way of choosing. We do not know why Mary was chosen. We do not know why God chose someone of such a humble context. We do not even know why God chose anyone at all. For there was no compulsion on God to require the services of a human mother. Nothing forced God to become Incarnate. There was nothing in the nature of the universe which decreed that God must come to the deliverance and rescue of the people God had made. No power external to God insisted that the second Person of the Godhead must live as a human, must suffer humiliation, pain, agony and must die at the hands of the very ones whom God had created. It was all God's sovereign choice.

The only constraint on God is the very nature of God's self. And that is the nature of Love. Almighty love is at the heart of God's process of choosing. And it is love, righteousness, glory, truth and grace which direct the choices God makes. It is God's grace also which enables us to be recipients of that love, which draws us, sometimes after years of reluctance, in willingness and unconditional acceptance. Then it is God's Spirit which takes our response and empowers us for our own calling, despite our great lack of qualifications.

For Mary was not the only one who was barely qualified for the task to which God had called her. None of us has of ourselves anything to offer for God's service. Our brilliant diplomas and important titles look unimpressive against the work which God sets us to do. Our athletic prowess or finely-tuned muscle look utterly inadequate for the race which Christ asks us to run. Our clever talks and brilliant publications sound trivial and shallow against the Good News which God asks us to communicate. We are all like Mary. We are at best 'humble servants'. For God alone equips us, God alone empowers and strengthens us. This is all the work of the Holy Spirit in our lives, and the Spirit is given freely to those of us who ask. So, as with Mary, our only real qualification lies in our acceptance of God's grace and love. The rest we need not worry about.

Called blessed throughout History

There is a wonderful historical awareness in Mary's song. It does not only call up the past, in recalling the promises God made centuries ago. It also reflects on the future. For these events that are happening now will be celebrated for centuries to come. And Mary herself is going to be remembered. From now on all generations will 'call her blessed'. Thanksgiving and praises to God will come both from those who know Mary, and from those who witness the birth of her child; but they will also resound through history, each time her story is told. Mary will be called 'blessed' quite simply because God has blessed her.

Although she has a very special story, and a very special place in history, Mary stands with other women in the

New Testament whose stories will be retold millions of times. For the New Testament writers as a whole have a thrilling sense of continuity. And other women who were significant in the life of Christ are celebrated and rejoiced over, and are an encouragement to us today. Sometimes even in the text there is the comment that this incident will be recalled, and this woman remembered.

One such comment is made of the woman who anointed Jesus. The story is told in some form in each of the synoptic gospels. In Luke's account of it the scene is at a banquet. Jesus has been invited to a meal by one of the religious leaders. In those days, many meals would be eaten in view of other people, who would be milling around in the nearby courtyard. This seems to have been the case here. For hardly has the eating begun when a woman from the crowd rushes over to Jesus at the table. In a scene of great emotion she caresses his feet, breaking open a bottle of expensive and fragrant perfume, and massaging it into his skin. She weeps and sobs over him, and her tears wash the perfume into his feet. Then she lets down her hair and, to the likely consternation of the hosts, she wraps it around Jesus to dry his skin. Those who had invited Christ clearly take a dim view of the incident, and without doubt would have liked it to be quickly forgotten. They are indignant and outraged that such a person should have brought confusion to their dining table, and muttering between themselves raise doubts about Jesus's own credentials for allowing, even encouraging, this. For me, the reply Jesus gives is marvellous. Far from accepting their reading of the situation he rebukes them for their own lack of hospitality. Instead he affirms the woman and points to her example of a deeply hospitable encounter, compensating in every way for the discourtesy shown him by his hosts. The 'beautiful thing' which she did will indeed be remembered, for Jesus promises that wherever and whenever the Good News is preached this story will be retold in memory of her.

And of course we are here to testify that this is indeed what happens. We listen today to the stories of these faithful women who loved God; these women of no status who poured out their worship of Jesus. For they remind us so deeply that God still chooses those of us who are insignificant, and of no repute. In her very person Mary embodies God's love for the poor and God's blessings on the meek, and we too call her blessed.

God still chooses humble people to be trusted as God's own servants. Because only those who are not full of themselves, those who see themselves as of no reputation, can give themselves up in the service of another. Even today, it takes humility to respond to God's call.

Prayer

Lord I often pride myself on being a good judge of character.

For I have thought a lot about these issues

And I can usually assess a human being fairly accurately.

And on the whole, when I have had to choose the right person for
    something

I have regularly made some very good choices

Of whom, of course, my husband is the most outstanding example.

And yet every now and again something happens

Which makes me realize I am actually not that omniscient

And that, unlike you, I am quite capable of getting things

Terribly wrong.

Questions

1 How much do you think external appearances affect your own evaluation of people? What other factors would be important for you?

2 How do you discover in your church whom God has chosen for which tasks? Are there ways you could do this better?

EIGHT

GOD'S GENEROSITY

LUKE 1:49

For the Mighty One has done great things for me, holy is his name.

All the way through her song Mary is aware of the *generosity* of God. There are no half-measures to God's goodness. Not only is there generosity in the way God chooses, it is there too in the way in which gifts and blessings are poured upon us. God gives in the way no other can, but God also gives in the way that few people are prepared to follow. Generosity seems part of the way in which the very holiness of God is conveyed. 'The Mighty One has done great things for me,' sings Mary, 'holy is his name.'

When we reflect on it this sense of divine generosity comes out everywhere around us. We are completely surrounded by evidence, even in the things we take for granted. Think how God has splashed out on colour and textures, on variety and detail. The thick greenness of the grass after a downpour in early spring, the vivid reds and golds in the sky as the sun sets dramatically over the lake, the rich purple of the heather on the Scottish mountains: they all testify to a God who loves beauty and generously endows the creation. There are no half-measures given to the butterfly. Fragile gossamer wings, breathtakingly delicate legs and antlers hover gently for a moment in a patterned intricacy of colour, and then in a whisper are gone. Or what about the peacocks, standing nonchalantly, contemplating the scenery, and then in one small movement fanning their magnificent tails in an effortless display of blue and green splendour? Sitting by my study window as I type this manuscript I am conscious of the tightly budded, fragrant pink blossoms coyly popping their heads through weeping and flowing willow branches as they compete to be the first to reach the open sunlight. There are cocky and idiot starlings gawkily flashing and scrambling for the food on the lawn, now frightened off by the swift landing and strutting of the black and white magpies. Beyond, I can see thick old oak trees, the strong slope of the hills, and the sweep of grey cloud in the afternoon sky. And this visual feast is but the tiniest part of the richness of the creation we live in.

Not only in the creation but in the Bible too we are showered with illustrations of God's generosity. They come out in Jesus' parables. I've often been struck by the fact that so many of Jesus' parables are about God giving banquets. In the story of the Prodigal Son the father kills the fatted calf and has a big feast to celebrate the son's return. Even though his son has been a waster and a layabout the father is undeterred in his generosity. The teachings on pride and humility are again illustrated by a feast. We should not go for the best seats at the banquet, Jesus tells us, but wait to be invited up higher. And several times the kingdom of heaven is portrayed as a feast: a massive wedding banquet. In one such parable the host has invited many people to come and receive rich hospitality. But the guests are not interested in this generous provision. Instead they are absorbed in the littleness and mediocrity of their everyday lives and turn down the invitation. Then the host sends out his servants to all those who rarely receive such invitations: to the streets and alleys, to the crippled, the poor, the blind, the lame, inviting everyone to come and eat until the banquet hall is full. In a very different parable God is portrayed as a vineyard owner who hires workers for the vineyard. Every three hours or so throughout the day he goes out into the market place, and finding people with still no work invites them to come and work for him. At the end of the day he pays those who have only worked for one hour as generously as those who worked all day.

The song about God's generosity echoes again and again through the biblical text. The psalmists sing about it, the prophets prophesy about it, and the writers of both the gospels and the epistles comment on it. 'He has scattered abroad his gifts to the poor,' quotes Paul in his second letter to the church at Corinth (2 Corinthians 9:9), 'his righteousness endures for ever.' 'If you who are evil know how to give good gifts to your children,' says Jesus, in the gospel of Luke, 'how much more will your Father in heaven give good gifts to those who ask?'

Even though God exudes a spirit of generous warmth, the society in which we live does not. There are so many ways in which we come nowhere near the kindness which we could show to others. In the parable, God invites to his feast those who sleep rough, those who are discarded and those who live on the margins. Yet we are often very reluctant to give anything to such people. There are always a hundred good reasons, we argue, why we should not. We are afraid of waste, of indulgence, of people not deserving what we give them, of scroungers, of those who laugh at our gullibility. We don't want to waste our giving on the phoneys or the layabouts. Unlike the generous Samaritan who picked up someone from the roadside in yet another of Jesus' parables, we are far more likely to pass by on the other side. We don't even share the sentiments of that Jewish rabbi whom a friend once quoted to me. He said he always gave to ten beggars, in the hope that one of them might be genuine.

This lack of generosity is not just an individual issue. Far from giving *to* others in neighbourly love, what is evident in our society today is the fact that people take *from*

103

others, in self-centred coldness. The ever-escalating spiral of fraud, theft, burglaries and embezzlement is a sad reminder that people are not out to help each other. Even the vulnerable and the elderly who have little find all too often that the little they have is wrested from them in violence and robbery. Nor do we see this ungenerous spirit simply in the incidence of crime. In fact, shopping in the local supermarket recently I was suddenly struck by the meanness of our whole modern materialist culture. Bottles, made to look big, held far less than the eye suggested. Impressively large cartons were only three-quarters full. Digital scales measured cheese, cooked food or mushrooms and priced them in hundredths of an ounce. The elderly man taking down a large can of milk told me he was sad that this shop had phased out the small cans, and left him with more to pay and more to waste. Smashed-up bags of crisps, damaged cans and a half-empty sweet packet, Sellotaped up, were being offered at three pence less than the normal price. Then, whenever there was any hint of generosity everyone had to know about it. The washingpowder carton bragged '10% extra FREE'; the ice cream counter announced 'No price increase!'

It is a long way from the example which God asks us to follow; that quiet generosity where the right hand doesn't know what the left hand is doing, but where both hands are encouraged to be cheerful givers. 'Give', says Jesus, in the gospel of Luke, 'and it will be given to you. A good measure, pressed down, shaken together and running over will be poured into your lap. For with the measure you use it will be measured to you.' Such images of reckless giving make our eyes widen. This is not simply an injunction to give a fair measure, and not to cheat. It is an urge to give far more than what is fair: to pack the quantity tight; press it tighter, bang and shake it till there is more space in the container, then pack it again until it runs over. And we are to do all this with a willing and joyful spirit because we are able to give.

Such giving has become so rare in our culture that we are both surprised and delighted when we find ourselves recipients of it. When we lived in Michigan, USA, I remember stopping at a fruit farm to buy a bushel of their delicious apples. There was a notice inviting us to munch and enjoy before we bought, which we did with pleasure. When it came to check-out time, the farmer, an emigrant Dutchman, and member of the local Reformed Church, looked at my polite basketful and laughed, pouring in three extra handfuls, and telling me not to be so mean with his apples! It was a warm and pleasant experience and one which encouraged us to pass on our own bits of generosity to others.

More recently, I witnessed another example of generosity which was quite different. Outside the Institute where I work there are several people who sleep on the street. They are now all friends of ours, and spend many of their days with us, often helping with the work, and sharing our meals. Each of them has a different story. Each of them, when at home in themselves, brings something valuable to our daily lives. Barbara has a wonderful gift of hospitality, and an eye for beauty, so can make the dullest room shine with joy. Gerry is an avid reader and fine pianist, and often brightens up our lunch hour tinkling the ivories of the grand piano. Charlie is a merry, friendly soul but has a drink problem and often doesn't look after himself very well. One bitterly cold night last Christmas when we were just beginning to get to know these new friends, Gerry came in, the chill and frost from outside evidenced on his face and clothes. He handed me a pair of warm woollen gloves. 'These are for that other chap', he said. He meant

Charlie. They were Gerry's own much-valued gloves. Someone had just discarded another pair in his direction, so he came quickly in to pass the generosity on.

Our culture is becoming increasingly one in which meanness is synonymous with good business, shrewd practice and safe profits. Generosity is 'uneconomic', unless everyone knows about it and it makes good publicity. Compassion too is 'uneconomic', because it gobbles up resources, time and energy. The sad thing is that when so many of the values of our culture are focused in this direction, it is hard for individual people not to mimic them in their own relationships. Those who feel they have received little can find it especially hard to give. When people have been victims of an ungenerous upbringing or lived in a mean-spirited environment it can be hard to be warmhearted to others. They draw a circle round what is theirs and live possessively within that circle. They fear invasion from without and erosion from within. And so they remain on the inside, with fists tightly clenched to keep hold of what is their own, unwilling to relax the smallest finger in giving to another. But a clenched fist cannot receive either, and it all too often crushes and destroys the good things it holds.

There are others, though, who have received plenty and still cannot give. They are happy to remain oblivious to the needs of others, and would rather set the dogs on the house-to-house collector than give something to Christian Aid. As far as they are concerned it is their money, and they are entitled to do what they like with it. Meanness is a baleful trap, leaving us holding on to something we barely want rather than part with it for the good of another. In the end it spoils what good relationships might be ours and what enrichment might come into our lives. Generosity requires the ability to let go: to break the circle, to ignore the boundaries and to open our palms wide before the God who gives. In that way we can both receive with pleasure and offer back with enthusiasm some of the riches from God's bounty.

Yet thankfully, even though the *prevailing* values of our culture might try to kill them off, many warm-hearted people are still alive and well in society today. I've noticed how a famine appeal draws very ordinary folk out of their own financial preoccupation, to give cheerfully, even recklessly, to those who won't survive otherwise. There are those people so moved by concern for other human beings who are starving, that they sell their furniture, or mortgage their house to help them to live. Charities everywhere report stories of sacrificial giving. Organizations which care for the well-being of children, or those with disabilities, or the welfare of animals, can keep going because some people dip deeply into their pockets and tip out the contents. As a result, people they've never ever met are provided for by those who care enough to organize an appeal. Folk who lack fresh water, or education, or all the basic amenities of life are helped by those who care enough to give. To be on the receiving end of people's generosity is like seeing the world with the sun switched on. It gives an altogether different perspective on the meanness of the rest of our culture. Frequently in our Institute we are filled with thankfulness and gratitude at those who support our work. Almost always they give to us at substantial cost to themselves, trusting that we will be good stewards of their resources. But more than just the fact of giving, human generosity is a heartening reminder of something else. It constantly reminds us that however much the values of any society try to deny it, *we are made in the image of God, whose nature is to be generous*. And when we show that image, and respond to the needs of others, we too find that we reflect in some small measure the God who is a great Giver.

Of course we image God only imperfectly. This comes out with gentle irony even as we give. Sometimes those of us who are most generous still have inhibitions. We find it easier, for example, to give money *for* the needy than to be confronted *by* the needy. Most of us can respond better if there is a trusted organization which uses and distributes our gifts to meet the need in people, rather than face it ourselves. The people who smell and are dirty and have little self-respect don't always excite our sympathies when we come across them lying on the pavements of our big cities. I have been with smartly-dressed, and generous, businessmen coming home from work in London on the Underground and seen them frown, and sometimes speak with impatience about those sprawling on the floor and making it difficult to pass by. Yet when later that night one of these businessmen writes his cheque for Oxfam, or for Tear Fund, some of the money he gives may well provide for folk like these. His generosity will be helping people in other countries who are also dirty and unkempt, and maybe lying out in the streets of big cities. It is interesting why we find it easier to cope with the latter more than the former. We can often 'sanitize' our giving, even romanticize it. Or perhaps it is simply fear or ambivalence which keeps us from accepting the man in our own gutters as someone who is also our neighbour.

Generosity is the measure of our openness to other people. And of course it is still possible to be generous with our money yet uneasy in our own relationships with those who receive it. If the spirit of giving is there, it is often all God asks of us. That may come as a relief to some of us. Because most of us are too squeamish, too afraid or even too proper to even contemplate doing more. It takes a

Mother Teresa of Calcutta, or a Mary Slessor of Calibar, to go and share the lives of those who have nothing. The wonderful thing is that there are many who do respond to God's call to do just that. There are people who like scrupulous hygiene and ironed linen napkins, carefully folded before lunch, yet have found they can overcome their repulsion and nausea and serve God in the mosquito-infested swamps. Generosity has taken ordinary, hesitant people whose hearts are open to Christ, into the drug cultures of Europe, into caring for AIDS patients in Africa, famine victims in Ethiopia, prostitutes in Bangkok, and street children in Brazil.

When Christians give generously of ourselves, we are confessing our trust in God. We are acknowledging that we believe that the God who had led us this far will continue to provide for all our needs. We are opening ourselves up in faith, abandoning our own neat and secure ways forward, and taking a risk with our resources and our lives. And that is one of the reasons why God loves a cheerful giver. It is a mark of our confidence in God's love, God's care for us, God's unfailing generosity.

Ultimately, God's kind of generosity is the willingness to give and not to count the cost. And each time we give we cancel from our memory what we could have done instead: the things we could have bought, places we could have visited, meals we could have enjoyed. In this way we image God too. For God is not a cost-counter. And yet God's generosity has proved very costly. In fact it involved God in giving up what was most precious. It cost the unity and closeness of the very persons of the Godhead. It meant that the One whom we call Father was prepared even to sacrifice the Son. It meant that the Son accepted a cruel death on a Roman cross. God's pattern of giving and not counting the cost is something we can never begin to experience, or even fully understand.

Yet it is in this great sacrificial act of redemptive love that God's generosity is united completely with God's holiness. We can join Mary's cry with our own voices: 'The Mighty One has done great things for me. Holy is his name.

Prayer

Forgive us, Father, when we close our hearts
To those in our world who are in need.
Forgive us, Saviour, when we take all too glibly
Your unstinting, costly, sacrificial gift to us.
Forgive us, Spirit, when we hide our pockets
From the urgent prompting of your call to give.
Forgive us, Holy Trinity, whose hand is always open to bless.
And help us to live in accordance with who we are
Made in the image of a generous God. Amen.

Questions

1 In the Old Testament tithing was seen as a way of giving back to God some of what we have been given. What methods of giving do you think we should adopt today? How do you organize your own giving?
2 What is the difference between being reckless and being generous?

NINE

GOD'S MERCY

LUKE 1:50

God's mercy extends to those who fear him from generation to generation.

My husband's grandfather identified one ingredient missing in the society of his old age. 'There is no fear of God', he quietly commented. I have reflected on its truth many times since. The absence of a respect for God affects much of what happens today. It is not shown simply in obvious ways, like the drive to make Sunday another shopping day, or the way in which the name of God trips as a curse off the lips of the smallest children. It is that so much of our public life is conducted as though God did not exist. There is no fear of ultimate justice or truth or goodness, because the God who gives meaning to these concepts is not seen as relevant to people's lives.

If we think of how God is presented in the Christian faith, and then look at the way our contemporary life is conducted, there is a sharp contrast. Indeed, if what the Bible says about God is true then it would send a shiver down the spine when we reflect on how nonchalant we are about the way we live. Most of the ambitious drive which leads people to stab competitors in the back ignores the warning that God sees all the thoughts of our hearts and the self-centredness of our motivation. Most of the malicious and destructive deeds, planned by merciless people in hidden corners, take no recognition of the truth that everything is done in full view of the Righteous Judge of the Universe. For Jesus himself warned us that what we do in secret will be shouted from the housetops.

In spite of these teachings about God, so much of our everyday life remains self-serving and self-justifying. Most of society has worked hard to obliterate the sense of a God who loves justice, righteousness and truth, and who hates evil.

Alongside this the Christian Church also seems to have lost the reality of the fear of God. This comes out in opposite extremes. For example, there are those who have become very 'pally' with God, conveying in their language, their prayers and their attitudes little of the reverence or awe which the former centuries of Christians exhibited. Instead, God is a chum, an old pal who can be relied upon to get them out of a scrape; a benignly rich uncle always ready with his cheque book to provide whatever needs their whims present them with. Then at the other extreme there are others who speak very loudly of the power of God and the judgement of God. Yet as we listen it becomes evident that they are identifying God's judgement with their own opinions. Their ideas, their interpretations are the only ones which must be heeded, for they alone speak for God. There are people who indeed see themselves as very close to God – but only in an advisory capacity. So when God rejects their advice, or does not heed their limited wisdom, they find it almost impossible to believe that they might have got it wrong.

The problem is made worse because when the fear of God has been invoked it has often been the wrong kind of fear. All too often the powerful in society have used the might and omnipresence of God as a stick with which to beat the poor or weak into submission. The nineteenth-century British gentry, church-going and dignified, sometimes misappropriated fear of the divine. Too often they presented God as on the side of the rich and landed and against the ruffian, the vagrant and the great unwashed. They also made God out to be a divine policeman, as comes out in an early nineteenth-century catechism:

Q. Whose eyes see you when your master is not by?
A. God's.
Q. Who sees people when they are pilfering tea and sugar and such things?
A. God.
Q. Does God approve of such actions?
A. No.
Q. What will God do to thieves of all kinds?
A. Punish them.[13]

In far too many societies we can see how the Christian faith has become associated with nationalistic ideologies. The name of God has been called upon as though he were a tribal deity, leading his people to exterminate others, affirming the political leaders and their policies, however cruel and however barbaric. God has been wheeled out to bless wars, to build up military strength and to promote national superiority.

These attitudes did not end with Hitler and the Second World War. In many quite unsubtle ways they can creep into people's thinking at any time. I have a personal experience which I found very sobering. I was in Los Angeles, jet-lagged, at the end of the 1991 Gulf War. Turning on the television early in the morning I watched with mounting horror a 'Christian' commentary on the events. Pictures of marching soldiers were accompanied by the caption 'Stand firm with the belt of truth and the breastplate of righteousness.' A shot of airmen releasing powerful, destructive missiles brought the heading: 'For we wrestle not against flesh and blood, but against principalities and powers.' And at the foot of a film sequence of exploding bombs and retreating planes we were told 'In all things we are conquerors, through Christ who loves us.' Nothing in the film honoured or reverenced the name of God. All that was evident was nationalistic self-congratulation, reinforced by an appeal to Scripture. The fear of God was entirely absent.

True fear of God is something very different from the 'ownership' of a deity who is always on your side. It is something far more humble and reverential. It is evidenced by prayer, by respectful waiting. Those who fear God are often brought to silence and obedience before the Almighty. For this fear is not born out of terror or threats, or dread of 'what might happen if ...'. It is fear born from deep awe and respect; from an understanding of God from the Word revelation and the Christ-incarnation. God, the altogether Holy One, is to be honoured; his name is to be loved, uttered only in prayer, petition and thanksgiving, not in blasphemy or curse.

Throughout All Generations

When I met my husband I was struck quite quickly by the way his large family's strong Christian commitment went back over several generations. Grandparents, parents, aunts, uncles, cousins were united not just in a celebration of blood ties, but very often in a fellowship of Christian belief. These links were there on both sides of his family. Plaques to great-grandfathers stood on the walls of the family church, and great-uncles had been preachers. Pictures of big family and church outings identified many youthful faces with unmistakable family likenesses. Twice had the Storkeys and the Stephens got together in marital unity. Older brother Storkey had married second sister Stephens, and youngest brother Stephens had married middle sister Storkey. My husband was born the eldest of the next generation, and has watched many of his younger cousins take the faith of their mutual forebears and make it their own.

Of course the family was not without its disagreements. There were temperamental differences, and theological emphases which made people in this close family sometimes critical of others. Yet my experience on becoming part of the family was of the long Christian heritage which was inextricably woven into family identity. My children's great-grandmother told me before her death that she prayed each day for every member of her extended family, prayers of thanksgiving and intercession. She prayed too that her great-grandchildren yet unborn would themselves know the love and mercy of the Almighty, and be brought into a living relationship with God. In many cases, her prayers have already been answered.

Just as those people in the Hebrew Scriptures were asked to live in obedience to God throughout the generations, so God's blessings to us flow down through the generations.

I have often heard children of missionary parents tell stories of God's faithfulness to them. They often link this with not just their own obedience, but the obedience of those who committed their children to God so many years ago.

Yet even though the testimony of generations is encouraging to hear, we must remember too that God's mercy is not limited to the generations of families who love him. Many people can testify to the fact that God called them and blessed them when no one else in their family background had shown any interest in the Christian faith. This was true of me. None of my grandparents, or the brothers and sisters of my parents, had anything more than a distant connection with the Church. A neighbour took me to chapel when I was a child, and then my mother reinvigorated her own church commitment and attended services with me. I must have decided even as a child that I wanted to espouse Christianity as a way of life. Yet in my late teens I met God in a newer, fuller way, and began to understand for the first time the message of the Cross and the reality of redemption. Mercy itself took on a deeper meaning. I realized in a personal way what those New Testament writers had spoken of centuries before: that God's mercy is that whilst we were yet sinners Christ died for us. Mercy became grace.

Real freedom is to live daily in the reality of God's grace. It is to know this grace in all our lives and relationships; to be able to pay back good for evil, mercy for vengeance, forgiveness for hatred. When we experience the mercy of God ourselves, we are more able to let this be an ongoing attitude of heart to others. And yet so often we find it hard. There is still fear in our lives, still self-righteousness so that the grace which God offers us so fully does not spread through all that we are. Ultimately our aim surely is to be permeated by the mercy and grace of God. So that we can know ourselves accountable to only One authority, and only One judge, and that judge is Love.

So often in the Scriptures we are encouraged to live in this freedom which God offers us through the generations. It is to our own loss and bondage that we choose any other way.

Prayer

Lord, what can be greater than your mercy?
Refusing to return evil for evil
Unwilling to annihilate the offender.
Allowing the sun to shine on the unjust as well as the just
Not giving us what we justly deserve.
Recognizing our weakness, pitying our pathos
What indeed can be greater than your mercy
Except grace?

Questions

1 What does the 'fear of God' mean to you? How can we help young
  people to distinguish between 'fear' and 'being frightened'?
2 What particularly good things have you learned from earlier generations in your family or your church?

TEN

GOD'S RELATIONS WITH THE POWERFUL

LUKE 1:51

He has wielded the might of his arm
He has shattered the proud schemes of the arrogant
He has brought down powerful rulers from their thrones.

Pride, arrogance and power get short shrift in Mary's song.
This same God who is merciful to the generations of God-
fearers is also quite ready to overturn the powerful, and
bring dynasties to an end. It seems that true fear and
respect for God are incompatible with human pride and
domination.

There are of course many kinds of pride. There is pride
that we often take in the work we do; there is the pride we
feel about certain people that we know. We can have legiti-
mate pride and delight in our children; we can feel good
and proud that we have overcome certain obstacles in our
lives. Not to experience a sense of pride and achievement
when we have just crafted a beautiful piece of furniture, or
cooked a delicious meal, or nursed a sick patient to good
health would be odd indeed. People sometimes protest,
'Oh, it was nothing really', when they are praised for win-
ning a match or doing very well in an exam. But we suspect
nevertheless that our praise pleases them, and adds to their
sense of well-being.

When it is tempered with realism about ourselves, and
humility before God, our pride is no problem. Taking a
pride in what we do is part of the commitment we need to
the tasks on hand. We respect our work because it is worth
doing well. We struggle with something because we want it
to be the very best we can accomplish. I used to love it
when one of my young sons brought home from school
something which he had made for me. When they were

123

very young it would be yellow-daffodilled cards for mother's day, or smooth painted paperweights done in careful detail and aided by an encouraging teacher. Later, it was to be a large enamelled key ring (I always lose keys), or a nesting box for the blue-tits (watching garden birds gives me enormous pleasure). Later still it would be something involving sophisticated computer technology (one year our first home computer had been carefully programmed to sing me 'Happy Birthday' after our middle son had left for school). I would often be warned some days in advance that 'it' was almost finished (although because I like surprises none of them would ever say what 'it' was). Then home would come the pleasure-giving parcel, taken excitedly out of a grubby rucksack. The expression of pride and anticipation on the face of the small gift-bearer was to me incomparably precious, and as great a gift as anything the wrappings could contain.

The pride that shows we care enough to be creative and painstaking in what we do is not the pride which Mary's song is warning us against. It is an intrinsic part of our humanness, it is our joyful response to the world which God has placed us in. We can have pride too in others, in the good they do and in their contribution to our lives. This was evident even with Elizabeth when she greeted her cousin's arrival: she was both humbled and proud that 'the mother of my Lord should come to me'. And we may also quite legitimately have pride and pleasure in ourselves as part of the very creation which God has made, and which God has gifted so generously.

No, the problem kind of pride is that which becomes *obsessed* with itself. It turns inwards, becoming self-congratulatory, living in and on the adulation of others. It is a pride which, in its grip on a person, obliterates God and so loses contact with reality. This kind of pride drives people to strive ceaselessly on their own behalf. It is often harnessed to a grim determination to succeed, often at the expense of other people. It fears humiliation; it fears failure. It is always bent on proving something. Any cost becomes worth paying, because *pride* is at stake.

I have come into contact many times with this kind of obsessiveness about one's own importance. I always feel uneasy when I am with such a person. Suddenly I am aware that this relationship is a disturbed one. The conversation is not open. The sharing is not real. For this person is *competing* with me, forcing me into a role I am disinclined to play. There is a catalogue of details which are meant to impress me. Honours and accomplishments drop nonchalantly into conversation: people he knows, places he has been invited to. His aces are always being brought out to trump my imaginary queens. When in the end I sadly give up and move to someone who is less troubled by her image and more ready to be real, I catch the look of satisfaction in his face, for he has 'won' the contest.

In a casual social setting these attitudes simply prevent any possibility of a congenial encounter, but in a more structured relationship they can be very destructive. Within a marriage, pride can set up patterns where one or both partners must always be right, and where it becomes difficult to admit to being wrong. Within families it can lead to alienation or isolation as some members are caught up within themselves and the others feel used or abused, but not valued. At work, it can lead to competitiveness, backstabbing, manipulation, where anything is justified so long as that person's will is asserted. In positions of high responsibility, or political decision-making, it can lead to cover-ups, refusals to step down and sometimes outright injustice.

For pride blinds us to our own desperate neediness, and holds us in bondage to appearances. It grabs at authority and power, and ruthlessly asserts its own will. At its most arrogant, it assumes ultimate authority and forces others into subjection. It is no wonder that this kind of pride is an offence to God, and that God acts with strength against it.

Pride and political power

When pride goes hand in hand with political, or religious, power then this is the stuff that dictatorships are made of. And Mary, with her prophetic insight, is quite clear what happens to them. God brings down the mighty from their thrones. God removes them from their palaces. This was true of many such rulers in the Old Testament, who asserted their power over vulnerable people. Autocratic dictators from the Pharaohs of Egypt to King Nebuchadnezzer had experienced an abrupt ending to their authority. The songs of celebration sung by the people of Israel, were often songs of release from captivity and from the domination of these powerful tyrants. The messages were clear: God alone is the Mighty One, and those who set themselves up as despots are contending against the power of God. It is sobering to look back on those ancient dynasties and empires of old and wonder whatever became of them: the Assyrians, Hittites, Egyptians, Babylonians, Persians. Many are lost without trace.

Mary's song is prophetic on this point in a very personal way also. There is a hidden poignancy in the words she utters. For she herself is going to suffer at the hands of the powerful. Those who still wield earthly power, who have not yet been pulled down from their thrones, will bring grief to Mary's own life. Against her choosing she will suffer through the tragedy of children. She is to suffer from Herod who will slaughter all the baby boys because of some imaginary political threat to his ruthless dominance. There will be that night of awful fear, discomfort and haste as Joseph takes her and her baby to flee from Herod's rage. Then she is to suffer from Pontius Pilate, who will refuse to take up the power that is legally his to prevent the execution of a just man. The injustice of an ineffectual Roman Governor will be the last sequence in an event which will pierce Mary's heart to a depth of sorrow. The injustice, the evil use of power, the abnegation of responsibility: these are all words which contribute to the agony of her devotion. But what it will all show her is that the powerful are weak. Their power is ephemeral, built on shaky foundations. Herod's power is so brittle that it can seemingly only be kept intact by the butchery of innocent babies. Pilate's power is so superficial that it can only be maintained if he washes his hands of justice. Already in her song Mary knows that real power belongs to God alone, and these others are mere usurpers. In the years to come, she will know it in her own experience also.

*

Through the ages there have been those who thought they had authority enough to control the universe: absolute rulers, surrounded by those who feared them yet who wanted also to be part of the action. There have been absolute rulers down the centuries, and many of them have been tyrants. Men (nearly always) of ambition, of hatred and callous indifference to suffering have peppered history with acts of barbarism and violence. Millions lie in unmarked graves as a silent testimony to the wickedness of those who have ruled with cruelty and vengeance. The whole pattern of such rulers staying in control, reeks of death and corruption. Bloodbaths, purges, vendettas, perpetual revolutions have gone hand in hand with doling out favours and privileges to people whose deeds were evil. Ideologies are the ones imposed by the regime. Truth is a matter of diktat. Yet the testimony of history is also that such rulers are often defeated. Some of those who have lived by the sword die by the sword, and their kingdoms are divided. Even in our own lifetime we have seen the toppling of such powers and dominions. Hitler's master plan for Europe – the creation of an ethnically 'pure' Aryan race and the extermination of the Jews – was certainly the product of a mind obsessed with its own power. His atrocities and savagery have left their scars deep in the souls of so many people and still create fresh wounds today. Yet Hitler failed, he died defeated, committing suicide, and the evil regime he perpetuated came ultimately to nothing. Since then many other regimes throughout the world have followed suit. History testifies to the truth that though absolute power might corrupt absolutely, it doesn't stay in business.

It is not always great rulers whom God pulls down from their throne, however. Sometimes it is petty tyrants, small-time leaders. Self-opinionated bureaucrats or people with no vision, who crush the weak by tons of red tape, can find that they too have their 'empires' withdrawn. A friend of mine was distressed at new by-laws which penalized the local vagrants. 'We don't bury the dead in our area any more,' he commented, 'we put them on the county council and they run life for the living!'

But just as not all pride is wrong, so not all power is wrong. It is only the self-confessed mighty whom God tears down from their thrones. It is only those who show a faceless lack of compassion, or tyranically build up their own empire, who find their rule diminishing and their arrogance blown away. There is also servant-power, however.

And those who use their authority in the service of others have the blessing of God.

When leaders see themselves also as under law, and under justice, then there is much less chance of corruption. When monarchs pay taxes, and members of the ruling elite are brought before the courts to face driving charges, or fraud trials, then there are already the safeguards and protections against the abuse of power. When legislation is in the hands of those who are chosen by all the people, and when patterns of firm accountability are set up, there is a greater possibility that power will be restrained, and people treated impartially.

Even democracy is not foolproof of course, and patterns of injustice, corruption and abuse of authority occur in most societies. It is something to do with human sin. It seems also that in all societies it is difficult for political leaders to admit to being wrong; they always have so much face to lose. Yet servant-power recognizes that people will get it wrong. What is important is that they see themselves as they are. They are not to be arrogant and self-seeking. For true office is held under the authority of God, and decisions are made in the shadow of the Almighty, and those who know this have a much humbler hold on power.

Prayer

You must have seen the palace at Versailles, Lord?
It's unbelievably grand,
Dripping in opulence
Every stone in perfect symmetry,
Every tree planted with an eye to its effect.
I couldn't count the number of marble statues
And every one of them a year's work for someone
Plus all the effort to get them in place
And then there's the gardens, magnificent,
The lakes, with ornate fountains, which all had to play at the same
    time
(They told me Louis XIV had the local waterways re-routed
To make sure the pressure would always be right.)
In fact the whole thing was built to pay homage to the Sun King
The powerful, all-important monarch who said, 'The State Is Me.'
It was good of you to put up with his delusions of grandeur, Lord.
Of course, he's dead now.

Questions

1 What do you think attracts people to power, and why do you think
   it can be dangerous?
2 In Mary's Song, why does God bring down the proud and arrogant?

ELEVEN

GOD'S RESPECT FOR THE VULNERABLE

LUKE 1:52

But has lifted up those who were low

In his fascinating traveller's guide to Godzone, Michael Riddell explains the topsy-turvy nature of God's edition of *Who's Who*: 'The small and weak and vulnerable are the most highly regarded. The clever and powerful and beautiful can look out for themselves.' Travellers in this heartland, being in tune with the heart of God, understand this instinctively.[14]

Lifting up those who are low seems to be one of God's characteristics. For all the reasons we have just seen, God draws close to those who are vulnerable. But in order to appreciate God's closeness we have to know our vulnerability. Those who go to great lengths to persuade themselves and others that they are impenetrable towers of strength, well protected from anything which might assail them, are going to find it difficult to accept God's offer of help.

There are many ways in which people can be 'low', possibly even more today than in Mary's time. We use the term to cover everything from being a person of poor moral fibre, to being someone who suffers intense depression. Yet, whichever way we think of the term, so many people in the gospels who encountered Jesus most satisfyingly could be described in this way.

Some of the people then were low because they had no status. Amongst these were women, the handicapped, the disease-ridden, people on the fag-ends of respectable society. Those people who were best kept out of sight, Jesus drew into the open to affirm and encourage them. For example, there was the woman with the menstruation problem, who should not have been in the crowd, defiling a Jewish rabbi, according to the customs of that time. Yet she touches the hem of Jesus' cloak and is healed, and rather than allowing her to slip away unnoticed Jesus forces her to speak to him personally and explain in front of the crowd what has happened. The result is that she hears from Jesus words of peace and affirmation, that what she has just done in faith has made her whole. Or there was the dreaded tax collector, much hated and despised and not welcome in anyone's company. He climbs a tree, tourist-like, to watch Jesus go past. The result is that Jesus calls him down, speaks words of love and welcome, and invites himself to the tax-man's home for some hospitality.

Some of the people then were low too because of illness or handicap. People who had no sight, the lame, those who suffered from horrible diseases, all found love and compassion in Mary's Son. There was the man with kind friends who were prepared to take him to the house where Jesus was staying, and drop him gently through the roof because there were crowds blocking the doorway. There was the man blind from birth, who found that a mudpack from Christ on his eyes brought light and then sight. Wherever Christ went, those who knew their desperate need reached out to him and had it met.

But not all of those whom Jesus lifted up were low in status. Some were in positions of great authority. A man in charge of the military was brought low because of the illness of a trusted servant, and came to ask for help. A rich man and his family were lifted up by Jesus as he restored to them their dead child whom they loved dearly. Those who were low in spirit, grief-stricken or overwhelmed by a sense of failure, all found in this Healer one who respected those who admitted their vulnerability. God loves those who are humble enough to admit their need and come to him with hands open ready to receive blessing.

The reassuring thing about a relationship with God is that we cannot lose face. Admitting what we are really like costs nothing, for God knows us well. All our weaknesses are already understood, all our pains and deep areas of hurt which no one else sees in us, are known to the great Healer. Our vulnerability is safe indeed in God's hands, for there we have nothing to prove.

Mary's song tells us how God loves those who neither bathe in the limelight nor hide their frailty and need. And of course Mary herself is one of them. She demonstrates in her own person as well as in her song that God chooses the weak things of the world to confound the strong.

So Mary can sing with integrity and with personal conviction. She can declare the Good News to others precisely because she has already experienced it herself. This young Jewish peasant girl, and her gentle, just carpenter husband, could not provide a greater contrast to the mighty arrogant despots whom God loves to topple.

I often reflect on the husband of Mary, for he must be one of the great hidden heroes of all time. When men are supposed to exude masterly dominance and leave their mark on history, he takes a very definitely backstage role. He shadows Mary throughout the gospels, yet acts with his own faith and trust in the goodness and wisdom of God. From the start he had a difficult task. He must have wondered whatever he was taking on when he listened to the angel and took Mary as his wife. He had to face up to his own pride and reluctance to accept this woman. He had to trust the message of the angel and be loyal and caring towards his young wife as she brought into the world a baby whom he had not fathered, in circumstances which he could hardly have chosen. No one wants his wife to give birth in a cowshed. Then so soon after the birth the kind Joseph would have to take his wife and their vulnerable new baby on a difficult journey to avoid the ugliness of Herod's fear and hatred. As the prophet Joel had foretold of times to come, Joseph was to see visions and dream dreams. He was also to remain insignificant in all worldly terms. Joseph must have been in every way a remarkable man: content to stay in the background, content to serve his wife in her great needs, providing what he could of strength and gentleness, content to search for his twelve-year-old boy lost after three days on a journey, content to apprentice his son patiently to pass on his skills and watch him develop into a fine carpenter, only to lose him from the family business.

The essential point about Joseph was that he was God's man for a very important job in the kingdom. And what that job took was humility. The servanthood of Joseph was to anticipate the servanthood of the One who for all those years had lived as his son. For Jesus, the boy, had been subject to his parents, and Joseph had taught him by love and example something very deep about the servant role he was to play.

The Mary who respects her husband, visits her cousin, and cares for her children is indeed one of those humble people whom God has raised up. She announces in her own life the importance to God of the insignificant and ordinary person. But the lifting up of Mary was not to a place of earthly power. God does not lift up those who are low to satisfy the world's ideas of importance. God lifts people up to a place of God's satisfaction, where their lives can be enriched and blessed, and where they are more enabled to reach out and serve others. Mary was not to be changed into a queen, or a goddess. She would spend the rest of her life in service, looking after those she loved, and being looked after by them in turn.

Our own ambitions must surely be similar. We need to be those 'little people', ready to become poor for the sake of God, ready to allow divine love to lift us on to new plains of relationship. But we are also to serve others; to be friends of those who feel excluded and marginalized and at the end of their human resources. Our own active compassion can show, more than the most elegant sermon, what God is like and how God meets the vulnerable in a place of safety and peace. But we are also to be active in other ways. Those who identify with Christ identify with both his compassion and his love of justice. People who believe what Mary sings can't, as one writer says passionately, 'sit on their hands and watch whilst the weak are exploited, the different excluded, the powerless enslaved.'[15]

If we agree with him, there is no shortage of concerns waiting for our attention.

Prayer
I passed a woman today, Lord,
Who thought I hadn't noticed her
And who looked away quickly
So as not to cause me embarrassment.
It was only when she had passed
That I recalled that I knew her
For she had once shared with me
A precious moment of achievement in her life.
She had changed quite a bit since those days
Become shabbier,
Lost some teeth
But she was unmistakably the person I knew.
So I turned back and called her name
And in that second saw how very much you valued her.
And I was rewarded by the pleasure of her smile
At being remembered
Even by someone so absent-minded.

Questions

1 Can you name some incidents in the Gospels where Jesus demonstrates how God values those who are vulnerable?

2 Who are the most vulnerable in our society today? Where do you think our society falls short in its care for them?

TWELVE

GOD'S COMPASSION ON THE HUNGRY

LUKE 1:53

He has filled the hungry with good things

Once again Mary takes up a theme that is part of her long Jewish heritage. She sings with the Psalmist of old, recalling what was written in Psalm 107: 'For he satisfies the thirsty and fills the hungry with good things' (verse 9). Another psalm echoes the same point: 'He upholds the cause of the oppressed and gives food to the hungry' (Psalm 146:7). It seems that God enjoys doing things in twos. Lifting up those who are vulnerable, and feeding people who know what hunger pangs are all about, seem regularly to go hand in hand.

For the people of Israel, God was indeed a God who fed the hungry. Often it was in quite miraculous ways. In the desert, where as even the youngest child at primary school knows, there isn't any food, God still fed the people. The miracle of manna, the beautiful, fresh honey-sweet wafers which God dropped on the ground each day except the sabbath, was a reminder to them all that this was a God who could be trusted. The miracle of the rock of Horeb, which brought out water for the grumbling Israelites who were slow to heed the reminders and give God their trust, proved the point once again.

Miraculous feeding was a demonstration of a God who cared whether or not people suffered. And it was not limited to the daily rations in the desert. It was there too when the rains failed and there was famine. A poor widow, who took Elijah into her home when she and her son were down to their last piece of bread, found the miracle of God's provision. Although it was used every day, her jar of flour was not used up and her jug of oil did not run dry.

Yet the song even here is not only recalling the greatness of God in the past. Prophetically again, Mary is singing of events which are still to come, events which she will witness with her own eyes. For her beloved Son is to produce many miracles of feeding. He will tell a few tired fishermen, who have toiled all night and caught nothing, to throw their nets out once more, to do what they know is ridiculous, and use up their precious energy. But something in his manner will draw a response from them, and they will know when the great catch is brought ashore, that following this miracle-worker, not mending nets, will be their life from then on.

There will be a wedding feast where a generous but careful host has under-catered with the wine, and begins to look a fool as the guests are still celebrating, and unready to go home. But the Son of Mary will accept the concerns of his mother, and ordinary water in big earthenware vessels will be turned into wine. And the guests will be amazed that so perfect a vintage should be left to the very end of the festivities.

There will be a crowd on the hillside, of thousands of people, women, men and children who have followed Mary's Son all day, and who hang on to his every word. For that word is life. And they will be a long way from home, and it will be late in the evening and they will be hungry. And out of a little lad's picnic hamper of two small fishes and five small loaves, packed by a loving, indulgent mum, the hunger of five thousand people will be satisfied. The Son of Mary who is the very Son of God will show the heart of God for those who are hungry.

*

It is not only with miracles that God provides food, however. Each day the creation gives what we need to renew our energy and replenish our bodies. There is that complexity of the food chain, the intricate way in which God feeds each part of the creation. There is the amazing renewability of the earth's resources, the cells that divide, the seeds that die to be born again for a new generation. The earth yields the richness of its harvest, and the young of all species find their food and sustenance in God's amazing provision.

Food is a necessity, a relief, and a way of ensuring survival. For human beings it is also a way of partying and celebrating. It is a means whereby we can care for each other and mark significant events in our lives together. God's bounty provides richly for all of human life.

Yet not all of human life receives what God has provided. And those of us who do receive cannot always understand those who do not. The reality of starvation and malnutrition comes to us only on our television screens. We feel uncomfortable when we see emaciated bodies lying pitifully in the dirt, but our own plates are full, and there seems little we can do. It is difficult sometimes for us to see how patterns of over-consumption in the wealthy world can contribute to malnutrition and poverty elsewhere. It is difficult to appreciate the part played by third-world debt, by cheap imports, or by low prices for basic commodities. As we listen on the radio to the plight of those overseas we often are eating or drinking produce which comes from those very countries where people suffer from poverty and disease. Yet we are grieved if the price of our coffee or tea goes up, or we cannot buy our dried fruit or nuts cheaply enough to make all the cakes we would like. We sometimes even decide to compete: growing our own sugar rather than buying it from needier countries. It is tragic when people starve. For in the world that God has made there is enough for all if we learn how to distribute it fairly, and responsibly. God ensures that there is enough for all who are hungry, but there is not enough for all who are greedy.

The responsibility of feeding the hungry falls on everyone. But those who love God are called especially to love their neighbour as themselves. The prophet Isaiah is not the only one to identify hunger with injustice, and to call upon the people of God to act with greater integrity: loose the chains of injustice, set the oppressed free, share your food with the hungry and provide the poor wanderer with shelter:

> and if you spend yourselves on behalf of the hungry
> and satisfy the needs of the oppressed
> then your light will rise in the darkness
> and your night will become like the noonday (*Isaiah* 58:6–11)

Jesus himself puts great emphasis on caring for those in need. In a dramatic account in Matthew's gospel he identifies those who love him with those who feed the hungry, care for the sick, give clothes to those who need them, and treat the stranger with hospitality. For as we do any of these things to others, we do them also to him.

Another kind of diet

It is not only bodily food that is implied in Mary's song. Some of those hungry who have been filled with good things may not have eaten anything at all. For there are many kinds of hunger, and we do not always know ourselves what we are hungry for.

There is the story of the traveller who was weary and tired and in a strange country. After a disappointing journey and a day spent in many fruitless pursuits he had a gnawing pain in his stomach. Knowing no one in town, and afraid of being ripped off, he followed a group of very ordinary-looking people into a restaurant. Ordering the biggest meal on the menu and half a litre of house wine he was surprised at the end of it to discover that he felt as hungry as ever. The people he had followed into the inn were laughing and making merry and seemed very pleased with the deal they were getting. He ordered another whole meal, and then another, and then, still hungry, he joined the queue to pay the bill in tired frustration. The party ahead of him, peaceful and satisfied, handed over their chit of paper, were embraced by the manager and left without paying. Bewildered, he handed over his own chit and complained bitterly as he paid the huge bill. 'I'm not even full,' he protested, 'and what about them? How come they managed to stuff themselves, and not part with any money?' The manager sadly handed over the man's change and then pointed to an item at the bottom of the menu. In translation it read:

Righteousness as much as you can eat: no charge.

Those who are hungry and thirsty for the right things, says Jesus, will be filled. He tells us '... do not worry, do not say, "What are we to eat? What are we to drink? How are we to be clothed?" It is the pagans who set their hearts on all these things. Your heavenly Father knows you need them all. Set your hearts on God's kingdom first, and on his righteousness, and all these things will be given you as well.'

The hunger that many of us have in our hearts is not a hunger that can be satisfied by things in the creation. It is a hunger that can be expressed in loneliness, in yearning, in a deep sense of restlessness. It comes out in something written by a sixteen-year-old student:

… just now I feel like crying, really it's funny, life is so beautiful and I want other people to enjoy it with me. It's funny, *here I am with almost everything a person could want and it's not enough. I always want more no matter what it is.* I keep asking people about it, but nothing, I get no answers. I don't get it. I feel like jumping for joy sometimes and then, like now, I feel like sitting down and crying my eyes out, but why?

Ronald Rolheiser who quotes that letter feels that it expresses something which almost all of us share at some time or another.

Whatever name we assign to this feeling, the experience is universal. None of us are exempt. Prescinding from more direct feelings of alienation and estrangement, all of us still experience within ourselves a certain lonely thirst. At the centre of our being an insatiable burning pushes us outward in wanderlust and eros, in restlessness and desire, to pursue some unknown timelessness, infinity and wholeness.[16]

God has put eternity into our hearts, and that yearning will stay with us. Although we can enjoy and be enriched by the beautiful things around us that God has made, ultimately our food must be of a deeper kind. Jesus demonstrates this in his own time on earth. He tells the devil who tempts him to a self-indulgent miracle: 'One does not live by bread alone but by every word that comes out of the mouth of God.' On another occasion when the disciples are urging him to eat something he tells them that he has food that they know nothing about: 'My food is to do the will of the One who sent me and to complete his work.' In his humanity, Jesus needed to eat and drink like everyone else. Yet it was not this that sustained and nourished him, but his relationship with the Father.

What *we* are hungering for is God, the Creator and Redeemer of the whole of reality. It is as St Augustine expressed centuries before in his prayer: 'You have made us for Yourself and our hearts are restless till they find their rest in You.' In the gospels Jesus Christ discloses himself to be the means by which we can fulfil this great yearning we have for relationship with the Almighty. In an amazing series of events, and to a wide variety of people, he identifies himself as the food and the drink which satisfies our deepest longings. To the Samaritan woman at the well he is the Living Water, and those who drink will never thirst again. To the crowds by the lakeside he is the Bread of Life, and those who come to him to eat will never go hungry.

We eat and drink then by feeding off Christ. We listen to his Word. We let his being and his truth penetrate our hearts. We allow ourselves to be reborn by the Spirit of God. We learn how to pray. We give ourselves to be remoulded into Christlikeness. We come together to rejoice, to celebrate. We seek the very mind of Christ, we seek God's heart of love.

Some of this we do alone, on our knees before God. But much of it we are asked to do in the fellowship and sisterhood of God's people. For Christ has put his followers into a body, and has given us a family feast to celebrate. Whatever we call it – 'The Lord's Table', 'Communion', the 'Breaking of Bread', the 'Eucharist' – it is so laden with meaning, so rich with truth about ourselves and God.

The historical context, the 'Last Supper', was a relaxing meal, where those who loved each other and spent time on earth together could rest together. Yet so much more was also involved. There was the sense of endings: they were beginning to realize that Jesus would not be among them for much longer. There was the symbolism of sacrifice: for Jesus is to be the lamb who is slain, the Passover feast, the one whose body is broken, and blood poured out for others. And there is the sense of beginnings, that what Jesus instituted here will pass through history as the love feast of the Church: the commemoration, the celebration, the reminder of what Christ has given for us. For Christ is to have a new body, the Church, where each member is asked to play a part in the service of all.

Today we continue that feast. But we do so in hunger for the kingdom of God and Christ's righteousness. For in Christ's body, the thirsty become the ones who serve, and the hungry feed others with God's Word of Truth. And we all are asked to work for justice for the poor, for integrity and wholeness; we are to work against exploitation and the abuse of others. And so we, as those first disciples, eat together, not just of the food of God's rich creation, but of the symbolic food of Jesus himself. Through his body, we become his body, and our act of eating together reminds us of our hunger for God. As we eat and drink we become aware once more how only Christ can quench the insatiable thirst of the world.

Jesus says: 'This is my body, which is given for you. This is my blood of the new covenant which is poured out for many.' And as we eat and drink, we feed on him in our hearts with thanksgiving.

Prayer

Thank you, Jesus, for your period in the wilderness
When you fasted for forty days and forty nights
After which, we are told, you were hungry;
An understatement, if ever there was one.
So when your Word tells us you care about those with no food
We can see it now in better perspective.
It is not only that your heart goes out to those in famine-stricken
    lands
And you want your church to share your compassion.
It is also that, even though you are God,
You know better than so many of us
What it is like to experience the gnawing pain of human hunger.

Questions

1 The feeding of the 5,000 is a very memorable miracle. What is there
about it which makes it stay in people's minds?
2 If God does fill the hungry with good things, why do millions of
people starve?

THIRTEEN

GOD'S SORROW FOR THE RICH

LUKE 1:53B

And the rich he has sent away empty

'There was once an American tourist who went to visit the Spanish author of many profound books. He was astonished to discover that the great writer's home was a simple shack filled with books. The only furniture was a table and a chair.

"Where's your furniture?" asked the tourist.
"Where's yours?" countered the author.
"Mine? But I'm only passing through. I'm a visitor here." "So am I," said the writer.[17]

In Mary's song 'the rich' are those who think they are here to stay. But they will find instead that not only do they pass through as quickly as everyone else, they also leave empty-handed. The first letter to Timothy makes a very relevant point: 'We brought nothing into the world, and we can take nothing out of it. But if we have food and clothing we will be content with that.' The trouble is that most people are not content with that. Some people are not content unless they have far, far more than that. And some are not content unless they have far more than anyone else.

'Godliness with contentment is great gain' says that same epistle writer. It is in fact greater gain than many other things which bring not contentment but bondage. When we consider the number of warnings which the New Testament offers us about the lure of riches it is surprising that we heed so few of them. It is worth reflecting why those who are rich might be in danger, and what it is that they are warned against.

First is the obvious point that the way people accumulate riches can be wrong. The prophet Amos pointed this out very clearly. The people he railed against had become rich off the backs of others. They had exploited the poor. They had denied justice to the oppressed. They had accepted bribes. They demonstrated in fact that all they cared about was themselves. In the New Testament James takes up the same theme. The rich he rails against have cheated their workers, living in luxury themselves whilst being unfair to those dependent on fair pay. But the oppression of the poor never goes unnoticed by God: 'The wages you failed to pay the workmen who mowed your fields are crying out against you. The cries of the harvesters have reached the ears of the Lord Almighty.' Ultimately, all that is gained this way will be lost.

Most weeks in our newspapers we read of people who get rich by swindling others. Over the last few years we have seen the Maxwell scandal, where a rich man became richer by annexing his workers' pension fund; the Barnet football club scandal, where the club owner took in the revenue, but failed to pay the players' wages for over a year; and the Polly Peck scandal where a business tycoon broke bail and fled the country rather than face fraud trials and see his wealth diminish. Insider dealings, shady transactions, syphoning off the profits, back-handed contracts are all examples of unfair play which inevitably penalize the honest. The demands of a rich lifestyle have traps and snares which can so easily bring corruption in their wake.

A second point is that riches lull people away from a real understanding of their mortality. In the parable of the rich fool, the rich man makes big plans for the future. Having benefited from a sumptuous harvest provided by a bountiful God he decides he can take life easy from then on. Rather than distribute his surplus to those who need it, he plans to pull down his barns and build bigger ones, and to live in comfort and relaxation for the rest of his life. But his life is going to be short, because in the parable God calls him a fool, and says that this very night his life will end. What then will be the point of his riches?

We hear of many people who are used to buying whatever they want. With a single piece of plastic, or a signature on an order form, they can have the goods, services, holidays, comfort, clothes and diamonds they fancy. The problem is that some are lulled into thinking they can also buy their way out of death. And, in fact, some do go to great expense to pay for the eventual freezing of their bodies after death, in the vain hope that at some time in the future when a cure has been found for their condition they can be resuscitated and a new life begun. Yet all that money can realistically buy for any dead person is a strong coffin and a hearty funeral.

A third thing to consider is that riches themselves are ephemeral. They are 'here today and gone tomorrow'. James points out that the wealth of the rich rots, moths eat their fine clothes, and corrosion eats away at their precious metals. We could bring this up to date and point to the way in which so much of our money-making activity is negated by external conditions. Inflation can wipe out our savings, fluctuations on the Stock Market can ruin our investments, recession can close our business, and changes in the mortgage rate can even mean we need to sell our house. One thing our modern Western world knows well is the insecurity of money.

The fourth point is a yet more poignant one, that riches bring us worries. The more we have, the more we have to worry about. If we have expensive jewellery or priceless works of art, we cannot even enjoy them at home. They often have to be locked away in the safe at the bank, because we dare not take the risk of having them stolen, and cannot afford the insurance premiums. For the more we have, the more we have to insure. We have to protect our homes with burglar devices, with cover-all policies, and sometimes even with guard dogs. It can be so protected that those who are rich become suspicious of anyone looking over their garden wall to admire the flowers. They fear the poor, and lose the art of trusting others or being able to enjoy casual relationships. And ultimately they can become cut off with their riches, surrounded by suspicion and hostility, trapped victims of their own possessions.

A fifth point is that chasing wealth takes us away from other values that are deeper. It fills our lives with anxiety, haste and suspicion, rather than leaving us with love, joy and peace.

A capitalist was horrified to find a fisherman lying beside his boat, smoking a pipe.

'Why aren't you out fishing?' he asked.

'Because I have caught enough fish for the day.'

'Why don't you catch some more?' the capitalist persisted.

'What would I do with it?' asked the fisherman.

'Earn more money. Then you could have a motor fixed to your boat and go into deeper waters and catch more fish. That would bring you money to buy nylon nets, so more fish, more money. Soon you would have enough to buy two boats ... even a fleet of boats. Then you could be rich like me.'

'What would I do then?' asked the fisherman.

'Then you could really enjoy life', the capitalist replied.

'What do you think I am doing now?' responded the fisherman, refilling his pipe.[18]

The story reminds me of a sixth point. It is that becoming rich can bring us more work. Not only do we have to earn the money to buy the goods, we also have to earn the money to pay for helpers to do the work for us to buy the leisure that we need if we are going to enjoy being rich! If we own a very large house, then someone has to clean it, maintain, service the equipment, keep the fabric up to scratch. If we own two big homes, it's twice the work. It's the same with cars, yachts, furs, antiques. In fact the same principle operates whatever we own, even if it is on a very small scale.

When our children were younger we investigated buying a magnificent climbing, swinging, hanging, sliding contraption for the garden. It was expensive, but very exciting: a potential present from generous grandparents. When I visited the shop and looked at the kit I carefully scrutinized the small print. After assembly of the two dozen pieces (taking several hours) there would still be much maintenance work. In fact every nut and bolt had to be adjusted at least once a week in order to ensure that the equipment was kept to safety requirements. With over seventy screws on the frame I began to realize what a work commitment we would be taking on, in lives that were already full of multiple tasks. We thanked our parents ... and threw a rope over the apple tree.

The final point is that riches can actually keep us from worshipping God. That writer to Timothy once again points to this. He reminds us of the temptations that come when we have our mind set on money, the 'many foolish and harmful desires that plunge people into ruin and destruction'. It is this author who gives the famous warning: 'For the love of money is a root of all kinds of evil. Some people, eager for money, have wandered from the faith and pierced themselves with many griefs'

(1 Timothy 6:6–11). The danger is evident. We can begin to trust in what we have, and that can become our ultimate security.

We can understand why Jesus himself told his disciples that it was harder for a camel to go through the eye of a needle than for a rich man to enter the kingdom of God. Jesus' explanation was penetratingly sound, we cannot serve two rulers: God and Money. That is why, when the rich young ruler asked how he could inherit eternal life, Jesus told him to sell all that he had and go and feed the poor. And Jesus' advice to his disciples is as relevant to us today: 'Do not store up for yourselves treasures on earth, where moth and rust destroy and where thieves break in and steal. But store up for yourselves treasures in heaven' (Matthew 6:19). For our hearts cannot rest in what we own; instead, those things can own us.

It is clear that where our hearts are there is our treasure also. And if they are in the drive to accumulate wealth and possessions the effects are both powerful and insidious. We live lives that are out of touch with the most beautiful realities of life. I remember some years ago being invited to a very grand function with lashings of good food, and excellent wines and spirits. The conversation was about this and that, him and her, and I discovered it was a sophisticated way of picking up gossip. The event took place in a luxurious setting, where heavy embossed velvet hung from huge windows, and pearl chandeliers sent fragments of light in all directions. As the evening drew on, and the room grew hotter, and faces grew redder, I excused myself from the noise and the gorging of food and drink, and slipped outside. A few hundred yards from the building was a small pond with a few ducks idly spending the evening light together. I sat down beside it, and for half an hour watched the most magnificent display as the sun slowly set, with its reflection in the water. The colours changed every few minutes, from subdued gold, to red, to crimson, to dark burgundy. The pond life reflected back to the skies the glory of the great variety of creatures who knew nothing and cared nothing about the material wealth of the people in the building. Feeling utterly refreshed and rightly peaceful I returned to the party, to convey to one of my hosts something of the glory I had just witnessed.

Rich and poor alike are human beings made in the image of God. Yet those who are driven to be rich are heaping up sorrows for themselves. And it is for these reasons that they go away empty in the song of Mary. They may well build up riches, but they have leanness in their souls. And God seeing their emptiness grieves at the short-sighted and fearful lives that people are prepared to live. And so it is with all of us. To put our hope, our trust and our faith in wealth, success or possessions is to set out on a dead-end journey. Until there is a sense of openness and a willingness to relocate our hearts and our treasures, no real contentment can come.

God invites us to have a light hold on material things. This is especially true if we are to serve God in our generation. For, as Henri Nouwen points out, 'training for service is not a training to become rich but to become voluntarily poor; not to fulfil ourselves but to empty ourselves; not to conquer God but to accept his saving power'[19] (Service indeed). And as another wise person once remarked: We are no fools if we give away that which we cannot keep to gain that which we cannot lose.

Prayer

We praise you
For you are the God of all riches
Every flower in the field is yours
And the cattle on a thousand hills.
Yours is the hand that carved the ivory
And planned its triumphant shape when the elephant was still an
    embryo
You are the one who shone the gold and placed it out of reach
Leaving it, idle, for human hands to mine.
Conceived the diamond,
Gave colour to the ruby
And thought up an intricate arrangement with the pearl oyster.
We praise you.
That being the God of all riches,
You save us from the perils of ownership.

Questions

1 Why is this chapter entitled God's Sorrow for the Rich?
2 Which of the warnings against riches do you think is the most powerful? And what aspect of being rich do you think is the most luring?

FOURTEEN

GOD'S FAITHFULNESS

LUKE 1:54–55

He has helped his servant Israel,
remembering his promises to be merciful
To Abraham and his descendants forever
even as he said to our fathers.

Mary ends her song with a declaration of God's faithfulness. God has kept faith with the people of the promise. To Abraham and Sarah, and their descendants through the ages, God has 'remembered his promises to be merciful'. And this has been a consistent act. However much others have been faithless, God has honoured the word given. For Mary's God is a God of *Covenant*.

A Covenanting God

The faithfulness of God is always presented in terms of God's covenant. The word 'covenant' implies an agreement, an undertaking, a commitment made by God. And it is an undertaking which remains binding, because it is part of the very nature of God to honour commitments.

Theologians point to the many times that this covenant is made or renewed in the Old Testament. Sometimes they talk of a first covenant being the creational covenant, made with the very first two human creatures. God gave them to each other, in companionship and mutual care, and blessed them with all good things in the creation (Genesis 1). Then there was the covenant made with Noah and his descendants, and all the living creatures who came out of Noah's ark, that God would never again allow any catastrophe to wipe out the people from the earth. The rainbow in the storm cloud was to be the symbolic reminder of that promise (Genesis 9). There was the covenant with Abraham, that his descendants would multiply, and fill the earth (Genesis 17). There was covenant again with Israel, through Moses, when God gave the Ten Commandments, and the people were returned to the promised land (Exodus 19). There was a renewal of the covenant through Joshua when all the people were assembled at Shechem, and Joshua reminded them of their history with Yahwe (Joshua 24). The covenant with Phinehas was a promise of priesthood, that the family of the faithful Phinehas would always serve Israel as priests (Numbers 25). The covenant with David was a promise of kingship, that King David's line would continue on the throne of Israel (2 Samuel 7).

But however we read this covenantal history, the important point is that the initiative is always taken by God. God reaches out to the people, and draws them into relationship. This is probably summed up most clearly in the Book of Leviticus where God promises: 'I will keep my covenant with you ... I will put my dwelling place among you ... I will walk among you and be your God, and you will be my people.' (Leviticus 26:9–13). The commitment is the Lord's, to be the God of the people, and to *dwell* among them.

The people of Israel had many *signs* of the covenant. One of course was circumcision. The cutting of the male foreskin was there to distinguish in an intimate, physical way, those who worshipped Yahwe from those who worshipped gods of the surrounding tribes and nations. There were also the signs of sacrifice. Young kids or lambs would be offered before God as a sin offering for the people, so that the innocent blood of the young animal would in some way be a compensation for the sins of the people. God would look upon their innocence and be reminded of his mercy. There were also the signs of justice, and right living:

164

the law, especially the Ten Commandments, were given to God's people, not to weigh them down with rules and regulations, but to help them to live in ways that brought health and peace.

Yet people had constantly to be reminded of God's faithfulness. In the immediate sorrows of life it is one thing that they were quickly apt to forget. Throughout the Old Testament there is a regular recalling of God's covenant with the people. And often, in times of hardship or unbelief, the people themselves are given the choice about whether they are prepared to continue as those committed to God. The choice, however, is only ever given to the people. God's own commitment is firm. And that commitment remains, even when the people are faithless, or wicked, or live in flagrant denial of God's love and care. God might 'turn away his face', or allow disasters and famine, but it is always in order to turn the people back to God, in repentance and a new walk with the Almighty.

The decision which the people of Israel had to face many times was whether to love and serve the God of their covenant or to go another way. For in the surrounding lands there were many other gods to choose from. Already there had been a precedent for deserting God when the Israelites had become involved with idols, during their wanderings through the wilderness. Moses had left them for a while to come before the Lord, only later to discover that they had carved out golden images, and begun a new regime of idolatry. The memory of that rejection of God was deep in the stories of Israel. 'Fear the Lord and serve him with all your faithfulness', urged Joshua, shortly before his death. 'But if serving the Lord seems undesirable to you, then choose for yourselves this day whom you will serve, whether the gods your forefathers served beyond the river, or the gods of the Amorites.' And then he concluded decisively: 'But as for me and my household, we will serve the Lord.'

When we come to the prophet Jeremiah, however, we see a very different kind of covenant. It points to what is to come. God unconditionally promises Israel that her sins will be forgiven, even though she has been unfaithful. But this time God will establish the relationship in a different way. It will not be through circumcision, or visible symbols. It will be by God writing the law on the *hearts* of the people. 'This is the covenant I will make with the house of Israel after that time', declares the Lord. 'I will put my law in their minds and write it on their hearts. I will be their God and they will be my people.'

This development is there also in another aspect of the covenant, that the Lord will *dwell* with the people. The author of the Book of Genesis sees it very basically. God walks in the Garden of Eden in the cool of the day and talks to the human creatures there. Later, we are told that God dwells in the ark of the covenant, which the Israelites take around with them. Then after the building of the Temple, God takes up residence there, and the high priests alone are allowed into the holiest of holies once a year before the presence of God.

But now, with Jeremiah there is a prophetic implication of a new sense of God's dwelling. This is fulfilled so deeply in the New Testament. With the incarnation, God came to live very physically among the people in the person of Jesus. And, after Pentecost, the Holy Spirit brought the presence of God into the very heart of each believer, fulfilling what Jeremiah had glimpsed, that the law, the promise and the Spirit of God will all be embodied intimately within human beings. And God dwells here with us even now, continuing the promise of the covenant.

All of this is recalled and anticipated at the end of Mary's song. The whole mercy of God is summarized, the promises of God, the remembering of God. God is a faithful, compassionate God, who does not treat people the way they deserve, but deals with them in forgiveness. And the reality of God's mercy, God's dwelling, God's *shalom* directs Mary in her outburst of praise.

But even here in her song Luke hints at a wonderful irony, because it is Mary herself who will take us from the covenants of the Old Testament, to the New Covenant. Mary will bring God home to the people in the presence of her Son.

Once again we must note how much this woman's life is rooted in Israel's history. She is enveloped in the distinctiveness and privileges which Yahwe has given her people, but also in its restrictions. In genealogical terms she has her place in the patriarchal lineage which the Israelites hold dear. She herself is to be married into David's line, the kingly dynasty who were special recipients of God's mercy. And the angel has promised that the child she bears will be given the throne of his father David, and that his kingdom will never end. She takes us through this history in her song. She takes us there also in her body. For the child within her is God's 'Yea' and 'Amen' to all that has been promised.

But Mary is of course also a *woman* rooted in Israel's history. She experiences many of the limitations of women in all patriarchal societies. The Hebrew culture has raised her status far above that which she would have experienced in the surrounding pagan societies, yet she is not on a par with a Jewish man. Like other Jewish women of the time, her word is not accepted on its own in a court of law. She has strongly prescribed gender roles. She is not allowed beyond the gentiles' porch in Herod's Temple. Her status may be higher than that of non-Jews, but she is still only a woman. She will be reminded of her subordinate position whenever she hears the prayer uttered by Jewish men, thanking God that they have not been born slaves, gentiles or women. Yet within Mary herself there is a new awakening. For this child will herald in a new era, a *new covenant*. And all those distinctions and restrictions between men and women *before God*, which have been taken for granted for centuries in so many societies, will through him be abolished. In Christ the whole of covenantal history will be thrown into new relief. There will be no more divisions of status between Jew and Gentile, between slave and free, between men and women. God is to 'remember mercy' in a way that no one has yet seen, and only few have dreamed of.

Christ then is to be the final fulfilment of the promise to Israel. God's mercy will be shown at its sharpest, its keenest and most poignant as Christ takes upon himself the symbols of the Covenant. The sacrificial lamb, the shedding of innocent blood, is to impart newer, deeper meaning for the Jewish Christians. The Hebrew believers will recall all the covenantal provisions of God, and know that in Christ all is fulfilled.

So, in singing of what is past, Mary is again singing of what is to come. God has remembered to be merciful. God has fulfilled his promises. In Jesus Christ, God will open up his mercy and grace to all, irrespective of their place of origin, or their religious history. There will be no more condemnation to those who are in Christ. For our sins will be forgiven, and God will remember them no more. God will dwell within us in the person of the Holy Spirit.

Call to Faithfulness

Prophetically, Mary speaks to the generations to come. Prophetically, she speaks to us today in the Church, for we are now the inheritors of God's promise. Redemption, mercy and hope come to us through Christ, for in him we are to live under the covenant of grace, and the promises of blessing. And we too are to recall and retell God's faithfulness in each time and era, each country and place, and to proclaim the Gospel of reconciliation.

Yet those of us who are in the Church feel only too keenly how unworthy and unready for this task it is. Sometimes it is only too evident that some of the tritest human pettiness, the greatest unloveliness, and deepest bitterness is to be found among those who claim to be members of the Body of Christ. Divisions in the world are understandable when people have not yet heard and responded to God's message of reconciliation, and the offer to be made whole. But when there is hatred, and scorn within the Church, then it negates the very *good news* we have to bring people.

What is evident is the need for a greater understanding of the mercies and grace of God. And this must not simply be an understanding with the mind, so that we can say the words together and know what they mean. But we too need that covenant written on our hearts, that we know in the very depths of our being that none of us is right before God, but that we all need to come to God in humility and faith, and receive the grace of Christ.

There is much work for the Church of Christ to do in this age. We have to proclaim redemption and forgiveness of sins. We have to bring healing and restoration and the binding up of wounds. We have to feed the poor, fight for justice, warn the powerful and the rich. We have to transform our whole culture so that the fear of God, and the glory of God, can be seen, even dimly, in our midst. And we are to do all this through the pathetic, faithless backbiting self-seeking human beings that we call the Church.

Thankfully, God has always chosen to work with those who are less than perfect, as well as those who are also despondent, weary and depressed. God is willing to have us on board even if we are full of uneasiness and scepticism, or if we find the whole Gospel lacking in reality. If we have fears which wake us in terror at night, or doubts which send us into numbed blackness, God is still the covenant God and can work with us. For even a bruised reed is safe with this God, and even a broken heart. Many of us have found that it is sometimes when we face up to our deepest needs and greatest sense of inadequacy that we begin to encounter the reality of God in a new way.

The message of Christ's love is that the Holy Spirit of God will supply all we need to live as the covenant people of God, if only we will come and ask. Wherever we start from, when we open out our empty hands to Christ there is a possibility of receiving the precious gift we most need. It may be the gift of warmth and caress; it may be the anointing with power; or a healing of the past. It may even be the gift of emptiness, and the knowledge that in Christ even that can be peace and blessing.

As very many ordinary people have testified throughout the ages, with our covenant God we can rise to heights unimagined. We can achieve miracles. We can pluck laughter out of sorrow. We can draw things that are precious out of waste and dirt. We can also come closer together in greater love for one another. Then, as the biblical writers themselves promised, people will know that we are Christ's disciples.

As we go into the twenty-first century we go with a God who remembers mercy and who loves us with an everlasting love. We go to proclaim a Gospel that is true and effective in all generations, and all millennia. We will not complete the work in our own day. We may not always know great success. This does not matter. For as one wise writer commented: 'Christ's Body does not need to finish its cultural task in a given generation; it only needs to be faithful with what it is entrusted.'[20]

Prayer

Our covenant God
Our dwelling place throughout all generations
Who through the ages past and present
generously repeats the offer:
I will be your God and you will be my people.
Help us sinners to enter into your faithfulness
That it might be for us a way of life
And that we might bring hope and love to a broken world.

Our covenant God
Our rock and defender, shield and hiding place,
Who knows the fears of our hearts
And the layers of inadequacies in our lives,
Take us, forgiven sinners, just as we are
To be enlivened by your Holy Spirit
And given the power to become
The people of God. Amen.

Questions

1 How can we best pass on the message of God's faithfulness to other people?

2 How do you think you might be a more effective member of your own church?

NOTES

1 Dick France 'Mary's Song: The Magnificat' in D. Wright (edit.) *Chosen by God* (Marshall Pickering 1989), p.39.

2 Elizabeth Ruth Obbard *Magnificat* (Darton Longman & Todd 1985), p.2.

3 Elizabeth Ruth Obbard *Magnificat*, p.16.

4 Henri Nouwen *Reaching Out* (Fount Paperbacks 1980), p.103.

5 Dick France 'Mary's Song', p.39.

6 Harry Williams *The True Wilderness* (Collins, Fount 1983).

7 Calvin Seerveld *On Being Human* (Welch Publishing 1990), p.67.

8 Elizabeth Ruth Obbard *Magnificat*, p.12.

9 Mike Riddell *Godzone* (Lion 1992), p.36

10 Ibid., p.37.

11 J. A. Fitzmyer *The Gospel According to Luke* Vol. 1 (New York 1981), p.307.

12 Dick France 'Mary's Song', p.41.

13 Quoted in Alan Storkey *A Christian Social Perspective*, p 395.

14 Mike Riddell *Godzone*, p.67.

15 Ibid., p.67.

16 Ronald Rolheiser *The Restless Heart* (Hodder 1989), p.66.

17 Mike Riddell *Godzone*, p.57.

18 Ibid., p.55.

19 Nouwen p.108.

20 Seerveld *On Being Human*.

BIBLIOGRAPHY

G. Bostok 'Virgin Birth or Human Conception?',
Expository Times June 1986

R.E. Brown *The Birth of the Messiah* (London and New
York 1977)

I. H. Marshall *The Gospel of Luke* (Exeter 1979)

Roy McCloughry *Men and Masculinity*, I.V.P.

Alvera Mickelsen *Women, Authority & The Bible*, I.V.P.
1986

H.H. Rowden (Edit.) *Christ the Lord: Studies in
Christology* presented to Donald Guthrie (Leicester
1982)

Sara Wenger Shenk *And Then There Were 3*, Hodder &
Stoughton 1989

David F. Wright Chosen by God, Marshall Pickering 1989

Mary Stewart van Leeuwen Gender and Grace, I.V.P. 1990

Memory card SD card

Storage carrying ~~pouch~~

holder wallet case   (cheap)

LED torch see 3 (£10)